Palestine History from the Beginning
To Present Era

Author
Ducas Ahmed

Copyright Notice

Copyright © 2017 Global Print Digital
All Rights Reserved

<u>Digital Management Copyright Notice</u>. This Title is not in public domain, it is copyrighted to the original author, and being published by **Global Print Digital**. No other means of reproducing this title is accepted, and none of its content is editable, neither right to commercialize it is accepted, except with the consent of the author or authorized distributor. You must purchase this Title from a vendor who's right is given to sell it, other sources of purchase are not accepted, and accountable for an action against. We are happy that you understood, and being guided by these terms as you proceed. Thank you

First Printing: 2017.

ISBN: 978-1-912483-54-9

Publisher: Global Print Digital.
Arlington Row, Bibury, Cirencester GL7 5ND
Gloucester
United Kingdom.
Website: www.homeworkoffer.com
.

Table of Content

Outline 1

The Environment 5

The People 10

History 13

The Stone Age and the Copper Age 13

The Bronze Age 17

    Middle Bronze Age 20

    Late Bronze Age 24

The Iron Age 27

    Assyrian and Babylonian rule 35

    The Persian empire 37

From Alexander the Great to 70 ce 41

    The Ptolemies 41

    The Seleucids 48

    The Hasmonean priest-princes 54

    The Herodian house and the Roman procurators 61

Roman Palestine 67

From the Arab conquest to 1900 75

    ʿAbbāsid rule 80

    The Fāṭimid dynasty 82

    The Crusades 83

    Ottoman rule 87

From 1900 to 1948 92

    World War I and after 93

    The British mandate 100

    The Arab Revolt 112

    World War II 121

    The early postwar period 126
    Civil war in Palestine 131

Palestine and the Palestinians (1948–67) 135

    The term "Palestinian" 138
    Diverging histories for Palestinian Arabs 139
    West Bank (and Jordanian) Palestinians 141
    Palestinians in the Gaza Strip 143
    The UNRWA camps 144
    Palestinians outside mandated Palestine 146
    Resurgence of Palestinian identity 147
    The role of camps 148
    The role of Palestinians outside formerly mandated Palestine 149
    The Palestine Liberation Organization 150
    Fatah and other guerrilla organizations 151

The Arab-Israeli war of 1967 and its consequences 153

    Israeli Arabs 154
    The PLO's rise as a revolutionary force 155
    The PLO's struggle for Palestinian autonomy 156
    Palestinians and the PLO in Jordan 157
    Palestinians and the PLO in Lebanon 159
    International recognition 160
    Palestinians and the civil war in Lebanon 162
    The PLO in the occupied territories 165

Negotiations, violence, and incipient self-rule 167

    The Camp David Accords and the PLO 168
    The dispersal of the PLO from Lebanon 169
    Years of mounting violence 172
    The intifadah 175

Tactics and tolls	177
PLO declaration of independence	179
The move toward self-rule	180

Outline

Palestine, an area of the eastern Mediterranean region, comprising parts of modern Israel and the Palestinian territories of the Gaza Strip (along the coast of the Mediterranean Sea) and the West Bank (the area west of the Jordan River).

The term Palestine has been associated variously and sometimes controversially with this small region, which some have asserted also includes Jordan. Both the geographic area designated by the name and the political status of it have changed over the course of some three millennia. The region (or at least a part of it) is also known as the Holy Land and is held sacred among Jews, Christians, and Muslims. Since the 20th century it has been the object of conflicting claims of Jewish and Arab national movements, and the conflict has led to prolonged violence and, in several instances, open warfare.

The word Palestine derives from Philistia, the name given by Greek writers to the land of the Philistines, who in the 12th century bce occupied a small pocket of land on the southern coast, between modern Tel Aviv–Yafo and Gaza. The name was revived by the Romans in the 2nd century ce in "Syria Palaestina," designating the southern portion of the province of Syria, and made its way thence into Arabic, where it has been used to describe the region at least since the early Islamic era. After Roman times the name had no official status until after World War I and the end of rule by the Ottoman Empire, when it was adopted for one of the regions mandated to Great Britain; in addition to an area roughly comprising present-day

Israel and the West Bank, the mandate included the territory east of the Jordan River now constituting the Hashimite Kingdom of Jordan, which Britain placed under an administration separate from that of Palestine immediately after receiving the mandate for the territory.

The name Palestine has long been in popular use as a general term to denote a traditional region, but this usage does not imply precise boundaries. The perception of what constitutes Palestine's eastern boundary has been especially fluid, although the boundary frequently has been perceived as lying east of the Jordan River, extending at times to the edge of the Arabian Desert. In contemporary understanding, however, Palestine is generally defined as a region bounded on the east by the Jordan River, on the north by the border between modern Israel and Lebanon, on the west by the Mediterranean Sea (including the coast of Gaza), and on the south by the Negev, with its southernmost extension reaching the Gulf of Aqaba.

The strategic importance of the area is immense: through it pass the main roads from Egypt to Syria and from the Mediterranean to the hills beyond the Jordan River.

Settlement depends closely on water, which is almost never abundant. Precipitation, which arrives in the cool half of the year, decreases in amount in general from north to south and from the coast inland. Perennial rivers are few, and the shortage of water is aggravated by the porous nature of the limestone rocks over much of the country.

For further reading on the political units most closely associated with Palestine, see the articles Egypt, Israel, Jordan, and Lebanon.

The Environment

Coastal lowlands of varying widths front the Mediterranean. The most northerly is the Plain of 'Akko (Acre), which extends with a breadth of 5 to 9 miles (8 to 14 km) for about 20 miles (32 km) from the Lebanon border in the north to the Carmel promontory, in Israel, in the south, where it narrows to a mere 600 feet (180 metres). Farther southward the lowland opens out rapidly into the Plain of Sharon, about 8 miles (13 km) wide and extending south to the latitude of Tel Aviv–Yafo. Once covered with marshes, the Sharon plain was reclaimed in the post-Exilic and Hellenistic period and is now a settled area. Fields and fruit groves are laid out between scattered sandstone ridges, on which villages have grown up. South of the spur of low hills that approaches the coast at about Yafo (Jaffa), the plain widens into a fertile region known in biblical times as Philistia, a district of orange groves, irrigated orchards, and fields of grain.

Farther northward the Plain of Esdraelon ('Emeq Yizre'el), formed by subsidence along lines of faults, separates the hills of southern Galilee from the mountains of Samaria. The plain, 16 miles (26 km) wide at most, narrows to the northwest, where the Qishon River breaks through to the Plain of 'Akko, and to the southeast, where the Ḥarod River which rises at the Spring of Ḥarod has carved the plain into the side of the Jordan Valley. Covered with rich basaltic soils washed down from the Galilean hills, Esdraelon is important both for its fertility and for the great highway it opens from the Mediterranean to the lands across the Jordan. The maritime plain connects with

Esdraelon by the pass of Megiddo and several lesser routes between the mountain spurs of Carmel and Gilboaʻ.

The hill country of Galilee is better-watered and more thickly wooded than that of Samaria or Judaea. North of the Bet Netofa Valley (Plain of Asochis) is Upper Galilee, with elevations of 4,000 feet (1,200 metres), a scrub-covered limestone plateau that is thinly populated. To the south, Lower Galilee with its highest peak, Mount Tabor (1,929 feet [588 metres]) is a land of east-west ridges enclosing sheltered vales like that of Nazareth, with rich basaltic soils.

Samaria, the region of the ancient kingdom of Israel, is a hilly district extending from the Plain of Esdraelon to the latitude of Ramallah. Its mountains Carmel, Gilboaʻ, Aybāl (Ebal), and Al-Ṭūr (Gerizim) are lower than those of Upper Galilee, while its basins, notably those of the ʻArrābah Plain and Nāblus, are wider and more gently contoured than their equivalents in Judaea. Samaria is easily approached from the coast across the Plain of Sharon and from the Jordan by the Fāriʿah valley. The city of Jerusalem has expanded rapidly along the mountain ridges.

From Ramallah in the north to Beersheba in the south, the high plateau of Judaea is a rocky wilderness of limestone, with rare patches of cultivation, as found around Al-Bīrah and Hebron. It is separated from the coastal plain by a longitudinal fosse and a belt of low hills of soft chalky limestone, about 5 to 8 miles (8 to 13 km) wide, known as Ha-Shefela. The Judaean plateau falls abruptly to the Jordan Valley, which is approached with difficulty along the wadis Kelt and Mukallik.

The Jordan Valley is a deep rift valley that varies in width from 1.5 to 14 miles (2.5 to 22 km). In its northern section the bed of the drained Lake Ḥula and of Lake Tiberias (the Sea of Galilee) are blocked by natural dams of basalt. Descending to about 1,310 feet (400 metres) below sea level the lowest land depth on the Earth's surface the valley is exceedingly dry and hot, and cultivation is restricted to irrigated areas or rare oases, as at Jericho or at 'En Gedi by the shore of the Dead Sea.

The Negev, a desertlike region, is triangular in shape with the apex at the south. It extends from Beersheba in the north, where 8 inches (200 mm) or more of precipitation falls annually and grain is grown, to the port city of Elat on the Red Sea, in the extremely arid south. It is bounded by the Sinai Peninsula on the west and the northern extension of the Great Rift Valley on the east.

The People

The social geography of modern Palestine, especially the area west of the Jordan River, has been greatly affected by the dramatic political changes and wars that have brought this small region to the attention of the world. In the early 21st century, Israeli Jews constituted roughly half of the population west of the Jordan, while Arabs Muslim, Christian, and Druze and other smaller minorities accounted for the rest. The Jewish population is increasingly composed of persons born in Israel itself, although millions of immigrants have arrived since the founding of the State of Israel in 1948. The Arab population is descended from Arabs who lived in the area during the mandate period and, in most cases, for centuries before that time. The majority of both Jews and Arabs are now urbanized.

According to Jewish nationalists (Zionists), Judaism constitutes a basis for both religious and national (ethnic) identity. Palestinian nationalists usually emphasize that their shared identity as Arabs transcends the religious diversity of their community: thus, both Muslim Arabs, constituting about 16 percent of the Israeli population, and Christian Arabs, about 2 percent, identify themselves in the first instance as Arabs.

The Arab majority resident in the West Bank and the Gaza Strip and the still larger number of Arab Palestinians living outside the area (many in nearby countries such as Lebanon) have strongly opposed Israeli control and have feared an eventual annexation of the West Bank and Gaza by Israel. Most Jewish

Israeli settlers support such an annexation and think those lands properly belong to Israel. In 2005 Arab concerns were partially assuaged when Israel completed its withdrawal from the Gaza Strip and handed over control of the territory to the Palestinians.

Both Zionists and Palestinian Arab nationalists have at various times since the 19th century claimed rightful possession of the area west of the Jordan River. The rivalry between the two groups and their claims have been major causes of the numerous Arab-Israeli conflicts and the continuing crises in the region. Some members of each group still make such sweeping and mutually exclusive claims to complete control of the area, whereas others are now more willing to seek a peaceful compromise solution.

History

The Stone Age and the Copper Age

The Paleolithic Period (Old Stone Age) in Palestine was first fully examined by the British archaeologist Dorothy Garrod in her excavations of caves on the slopes of Mount Carmel in 1929–34. The finds showed that at that stage Palestine was culturally linked with Europe, and human remains were recovered showing that the inhabitants were of the same group as the Neanderthal inhabitants of Europe. The Mesolithic Period (Middle Stone Age) is best represented by a culture called Natufian, known from excavations at ʿAin

Mallāha and Jericho. The Natufians lived in caves, as did their Paleolithic predecessors, but there is a possibility that they were experimenting in agriculture, for the importance to them of the collection of grain is shown by the artistic care that they lavished on the carving of the hafts of their sickles and in the provision of utensils for grinding. During the subsequent Neolithic Period (New Stone Age) humans gradually undertook the domestication of animals, the cultivation of crops, the production of pottery, and the building of towns (e.g., Jericho by 7000 bce).

Excavations also have provided a picture of events in Palestine in the 5th–4th millennium bce, during which the transition from the Stone Age to the Copper Age took place. It was probably in the 4th millennium that the Ghassulians immigrated to Palestine. Their origin is not known; they are called Ghassulians because the pottery and flints characteristic of their settlements first attracted attention in the excavations of Tulaylāt al-Ghassūl in the Jordan Valley. There was a permanent village site with several successive layers of occupation, and the site probably was associated with reasonably efficient agriculture.

The phase can be called the Aeneolithic or Chalcolithic Period or the Copper Age, since copper axes were found at Tulaylāt al-Ghassūl, and this is confirmed by the finds at sites near Beersheba, with pottery and a flint industry allied to those of Tulaylāt al-Ghassūl but not identical with them. At Beersheba there was a copper-working industry, which presumably imported ore from Sinai, and there was also evidence of an ivory-working industry, both proving the growth of a class of specialist craftsmen. Discoveries near 'En Gedi have revealed a shrine of that period, and basketry, ivory, leather, and hundreds of copper ritual objects were found in the Naḥal Mishmar caves of the Judaean desert.

The region in which the Ghassulian settlements have been found is mainly in the south of Palestine, with an extension up the coastal plain and its fringes. These settlements seem to have died out and disappeared in the last centuries of the 4th millennium, about the same time that a new population immigrated, probably from the north. Thereafter the composite elements in Palestine consisted of the indigenous Neolithic-Chalcolithic population, the Ghassulians, and these latest immigrants; in time the peoples were amalgamated into what was to become the sedentary urban population of the Early Bronze Age in the 3rd millennium.

Palestine's dating is henceforth linked to Egyptian dating until the time of the Hebrew monarchy; the interpretation of Egyptian dates in German Egyptologist Rolf Krauss's Sothis- und Monddaten (1985; "Sothic and Lunar Dates") is followed in this article.

The Bronze Age

Early Bronze Age

Most of the towns that are known in historic times came into existence during the Early Bronze Age. The growth of these towns can be approximately correlated chronologically with the development of the Old Kingdom in Egypt, Early Bronze I corresponding to the late Predynastic Period and Early Bronze II being cross-dated by finds to the time of the 1st dynasty, c. 2925 bce. Evidence of the early phases of the Early Bronze Age comes mainly from Megiddo, Jericho, Tall al-Farʻah, Tel Bet Sheʼan, Khirbat al-Karak, and Ai (Khirbat ʻAyy). All these sites are in northern or central Palestine, and it was there that the Early Bronze Age towns seem to have developed. The towns of southern Palestine for instance, Tel Lakhish, Kiriath-sepher, and Tel Ḥasi seem only to have been established in Early Bronze III. The town dwellers, identified as the original Semitic population, can, for the sake of convenience, be called Canaanites, although the term is not attested before the middle of the 2nd millennium bce. (See Canaan.)

In the course of the 3rd millennium, therefore, walled towns began to appear throughout Palestine. There is no evidence that the next step of unification under the leadership of a single town took place in the region, as it had in Mesopotamia and Egypt; Palestine's towns presumably remained independent city-states, except insofar as Egypt may at times have exercised a loose political control. By about the 23rd century bce the whole civilization had ceased to be urban. During the next phase it was pastoral and was influenced by the settlement of nomads probably from east of the Jordan River.

Among the nomads, Amorites from the Syrian Desert may have predominated. It is not yet fully understood how these events are related to the creation of the

Akkadian empire in Mesopotamia under Sargon of Akkad and his grandson Naram-Sin (24th and 23rd centuries bce) and to the latter's destruction of the powerful kingdom of Ebla (modern Tall Mardīkh) in neighbouring Syria, nor is the extent of Eblaite and Akkadian hegemony over Palestine in this period known. It does seem reasonable, however, to associate the incursion of nomads from the east with the invasions of Egypt by people from Asia that brought the Old Kingdom to an end. An initial date of 23rd–22nd century bce, depending on the interpretation of the Egyptian evidence, and a final date of the 20th century bce seem probable.

The picture of Palestine at this period is thus unequivocally that of a region occupied by a number of allied tribes; although they had many features in common, there were also many differences. The most significant point is that, with the possible exception of the northern group, they made no contribution at all to town life. The different groups had tribal centres, but they were essentially seminomadic pastoralists. This description fits well that given in the Book of Joshua of the Amorites who lived in the hill country, as opposed to the Canaanites who lived in the plains and on the coast areas favourable to agriculture.

Middle Bronze Age

It was, in fact, the next period the Middle Bronze Age that introduced the Canaanite culture as found by the Israelites on their entry into Palestine. The Middle Bronze Age (c. 2000–c. 1550 bce) provides the background for the beginning of the story of the Hebrew Bible. The archaeological evidence for the period shows new types of pottery, weapons, and burial practices. Once more an urban civilization based on agriculture was established. It is not entirely clear whether the wave of urban development after the 20th century bce was the work of a new immigrant people accustomed to town dwelling or of the local inhabitants themselves, some of whom may have adopted a sedentary lifestyle and begun, as in Mesopotamia and Syria, to establish dynasties. But where they settled, towns of the widespread Middle Bronze Age civilization of Palestine emerged.

This civilization was intimately connected with that of the towns of the Phoenician-Canaanite coast. Extant Egyptian documents provide valuable information about Palestine in the period of the Egyptian 12th dynasty (1938–1756 bce) and argue for significant Egyptian interest and influence in Palestine at this time. (Most notable are the popular literary work known as the Story of Sinuhe, detailing the hero's exile in the Palestinian region, and the 20th–19th-century "Execration Texts," inscriptions of Egypt's enemies' names on pottery, which was ceremonially broken to invoke a curse.) The culture introduced at this stage was essentially the same as the culture found by the

Israelites who moved into Palestine in the 14th and 13th centuries bce.

A large repertory of new forms in pottery arose, and for the first time in Palestine the clay was turned entirely on a fast wheel. Comparisons of Palestinian early Middle Bronze pottery forms with metallic and ceramic forms at Byblos, dated by Egyptian contacts, suggest that these forms were brought to Palestine about the 19th century from coastal Syria. Bronze weapons of a distinctive type, paralleled also on the Syrian coast, have been found at Megiddo, Jericho, and Tall al-'Ajjul. Town life in Palestine gradually expanded after the mid-19th century bce, but the material culture was essentially a direct development from the preceding stage.

Several towns of Middle Bronze Age Palestine were defended by plaster-faced ramparts (clearly discernible at Jericho and many other sites), an imported method of fortification giving evidence of a new and alien influence superimposed on the existing Canaanite culture. These were probably introduced by the Asiatic Hyksos, possibly related to the Amorites, who secured control of northern Egypt about 1630. The Hyksos may have included elements of a grouping of people, largely Semitic, called the Habiru or Hapiru (Egyptian 'Apiru). (The term Habiru, meaning "Outsiders," was applied to nomads, fugitives, bandits, and workers of inferior status; the word is etymologically related to "Hebrew," and the relationship of the Habiru [and aforementioned Hyksos] to the Hebrews has long been debated.) The Habiru appear to have established a military aristocracy in Palestine, bringing to the towns new defenses and new prosperity (as well as many Egyptian cultural elements) without interrupting the basic character of the local culture; this was to survive the destruction of Megiddo, Jericho, and Kiriath-sepher that followed the Egyptians' expulsion of the Hyksos into Palestine at the end of the Middle Bronze Age (c. 1550).

Late Bronze Age

There was no sharp break between the Middle and Late Bronze Age in Palestine. Shortly before the death of Ahmose I (1514 bce), the first native pharaoh of the New Kingdom, the Egyptian armies began to conquer Palestine, probably completing their task during his successor's reign. Under Queen Hatshepsut (1479–58) Palestine revolted against Egyptian domination, but the rebellion was put down firmly by her successor, Thutmose III, who established a stable administration, maintained through the reigns of his immediate successors. Egyptian administrative documents excavated in both Egypt and Palestine show in considerable detail how the provincial government was organized and even how it operated during the century 1450–1350 bce.

Documents show, for example, that the land of Retenu (Syria-Palestine) was divided into three administrative districts, each under an Egyptian governor. The third district (Canaan) included all of Palestine from the Egyptian border to Byblos. This period is often known as the Amarna Age and is vividly illustrated by several hundred letters written in cuneiform script, found in Egypt at Tell el-Amarna, site of the capital of the "heretic king" Akhenaton. The unusual concern of the pharaohs with the affairs of Palestine was chiefly a result of the fact that control of it was necessary for the defense of Phoenicia and southern Syria, menaced by Mitanni until about 1375 and by the Hittite empire after that date.

About 1292 bce the increasingly weak rule of the last pharaohs of the 18th dynasty was replaced by the strong arm of the second and third kings of the 19th dynasty, Seti I and Ramses II (1279–13 bce). These kings blunted the southward thrust of the Hittites and consolidated the crumbling Egyptian empire. The exactions of foreign bureaucrats, however, combined with internal decay, had so enfeebled the Canaanite vassal princes of Palestine that it was comparatively easy for the incoming Israelites to occupy most of the hill country east of the Jordan River and in western Palestine during the closing decades of the 13th century bce. Archaeological evidence suggests that the Israelite settlement in Palestine was much more complex and disconnected than the biblical accounts indicate. During a short interlude of anarchy that followed the last weak kings of the 19th dynasty, Egyptian rule was completely extinguished, and the ephemeral victories of Ramses III in the early decades of the 12th century scarcely affected Palestinian history.

Subsequent histories of the region have relied heavily on biblical narrative. Although this narrative has been augmented to a great extent by information derived from modern archaeological excavations and, for some historical periods, by outside written sources it is frequently the major, or sole, source of historical information; however, its validity has often been disputed.

The Iron Age

The Israelites in Palestine

Though the Israelite tribes entered Palestine before the end of the Late Bronze Age, they did not become firmly established in their new home until the early decades of the 12th century bce. Their number was increased greatly during the settling of Canaan by seminomadic Hebrew tribes already in Palestine, as well as by many settled Canaanites (e.g., the Gibeonites), who joined the invaders against their sedentary neighbours. Excavation has made it clear that the Israelites began building amid the ruins of their precursors and that new settlements sprang up rapidly all through the hill country.

Had events followed their normal course, the resurgent Canaanites, who had not been driven from the coastal plain or the Plain of Esdraelon, might have overwhelmed the scattered and unorganized Israelite clans, but this was prevented by the great invasion of the Sea Peoples in the time of Ramses III, in the early decades of the 12th century bce. Among the invaders from the Aegean basin were the Philistines, who were to conquer much of the region within a century and a half after their settlement in the southern coastal plain.

(The Philistines have been identified with the so-called Peleset, who were used as garrison troops and mercenaries by Ramses III.) Meanwhile, three other peoples were settling east of the Jordan River: the Edomites in the south, the Moabites east of the Dead

Sea, and the Ammonites on the edge of the Syrian Desert east of Gilead. Considered by the Israelites as fellow Hebrews, these peoples had begun to settle down before the Israelite invasion, and they remained polytheists until the end of the Hebrew Bible period.

The early Israelites possessed a strong centralizing force in their monotheistic faith, combined with a stern code of ethics, which set them apart from all their neighbours. The Mosaic tradition of the covenant between Yahweh and Israel, made concrete by the Tabernacle and its ritual, bound the tribes together in a cultic bond resembling the later Greek amphictyonies. Characteristic of these organizations was a central sanctuary, surrounded by its worshipers. Straining against this religious bond were disruptive tribal forces held in leash by a loose alliance between the tribes, which was often severed by civil war. But for the constant attacks launched by its neighbours, Israel would perhaps never have attained any political solidarity. As it was, salvation from its foes lay only in union, and, after abortive attempts had been made at one-man rule, Saul became king of all of Israel (c. 1020 bce).

Saul defeated the Ammonites and the Philistines but was killed in battle against the latter about 1000 bce and was succeeded by David. King David crushed the Philistines (c. 990) and conquered the three Hebrew states east of the Jordan River, after which the intervention of the Aramaeans from Syria forced him to defeat and annex the states of Aram as far north as the borders of Hamath on the Orontes River. Farther east he established some sort of control over the nomadic tribes of the Syrian Desert as far as the Euphrates River, though it is scarcely probable that Israelite domination was that effective. At home David organized a stable administration based largely on Egyptian models and, according to tradition, carried out a census of the population. He died before he could complete his plans, but they were put into effect by his successor, Solomon.

The reign of Solomon (mid-10th century) represents the culmination of Israelite political history. Though Solomon gradually lost control over outlying territories conquered by David, he was extraordinarily successful in organizing the economic life of the country. He joined forces with Hiram of Tyre, who was leading the Phoenicians toward the exploitation of Mediterranean trade. Expeditions to Ophir, a region probably in either East Africa or India, brought items of wealth such as gold, peacocks, and sandalwood to Palestine.

At the same time, the Israelite king entered into trade relations with the Arabs as far south as Sheba, or Saba' (modern Yemen). These activities would have been impossible but for the development of new principles in shipbuilding and for the recent domestication of the Arabian camel and its use in the caravan trade. Among the king's other undertakings was the construction of a fortress or storehouse at a site near the head of the Gulf of Aqaba. The modern site, Tell el-Kheleifah, may have been the biblical Ezion-geber. Most of the kingdom's wealth was spent in elaborate building operations, which included the Temple of Jerusalem and the royal palace, as well as numerous fortified towns.

The best-known of these are Megiddo, Hazor, and Gezer. But royal activities on such a vast scale cost more than was produced by foreign trade and the tribute of vassal states, and the Israelites themselves were forced to submit to conscription in royal labour gangs as well as to heavy levies of various kinds. It is not surprising that the people of northern Israel revolted after the great king's death, thus disrupting the united monarchy.

The rump kingdom of Israel lasted two full centuries, sharing the worship of Yahweh and the Mosaic tradition with its smaller southern neighbour, Judah. After a period of intermittent warfare between Judah and Israel, King Asa of Judah entered into an alliance with the growing kingdom of Damascus, by which the latter attacked northern Israel, thus relieving pressure on Judah. This move cost Israel its territory to the east of the Jordan River and north of the Yarmūk River and ushered in a long series of wars between Israel and Damascus, which did not end until the capture of Damascus by the Assyrians in 732 bce.

The best-known phase of Israelite history is the period during which the great prophets, Elijah and Elisha, flourished, under the Omrides of the 9th century. Omri himself, founder of the dynasty, selected Samaria as his capital and began constructing elaborate defenses and royal buildings, which have been uncovered by excavations. His son Ahab was alternately hero and villain of the principal stories of the prophets; he became involved in complex international maneuvers, which ended with his ignominious death at Ramoth-Gilead.

The dynasty of Omri ended amid torrents of blood (c. 841 bce); it was followed by the dynasty of Jehu, which lasted nearly a century. This was a period of extreme oscillations, from the catastrophic defeat of Israel (c. 815 bce) and the destruction of its army by Hazael, king of Damascus, to the triumphs of Jeroboam II (c. 786–746 bce). Meanwhile, Judah also oscillated between periods of prosperity and weakness; when it was strong, it controlled Edom and the caravan routes of the south from Midian to the Mediterranean; when it was feeble, it shrank behind its own narrow boundaries. Great kings such as Asa, Jehoshaphat, and Uzziah alternated with weak kings.

In 741/740 bce the death knell of independence in Syria and Palestine was sounded by the capture of Arpad in northern Syria by the Assyrian king Tiglath-pileser III. Events unfolded with dizzying speed. In 738 Israel and Judah paid tribute to Assyria for the first time in decades; in 733 the Assyrians devastated Gilead and Galilee, turning the entire land into Assyrian provinces except for the territory of two tribes, western Manasseh and Ephraim; in 732 Damascus was captured and Aram ceased to exist as a state; and in 725 the siege of Samaria began. Finally, in the first months of 722, Samaria was taken and Israel became politically extinct.

Assyrian and Babylonian rule

Judah was left the sole heir of the legacy of David and Solomon. Hezekiah (c. 715–c. 686 bce), lured by promises of Egyptian aid, attempted to resist Assyria but was defeated and compelled to pay a crushing tribute. It is possible that only the timely intervention of an epidemic that decimated the Assyrian army of Sennacherib saved Judah from total devastation. The eloquent guidance of the prophet Isaiah restored the morale of the people, and even the weakness of Hezekiah's son Manasseh did not bring complete ruin.

Another strong king, Josiah (c. 640–609 bce), arose in time to restore the ebbing fortunes of Judah for a few years, during which much of the ancient territory of united Israel was brought back under the rule of the Davidic dynasty. Assyria was rapidly declining in power, and in 612 its hated capital, Nineveh, was destroyed by the Medes. Josiah's successful rebellion ended when he fell in battle against a more powerful contender for the Assyrian succession, Necho of Egypt.

Meanwhile, the Chaldean kings of Babylonia were rapidly gaining strength. Nabopolassar of Babylon and Cyaxares of Media divided the old Assyrian empire between them, and the former's son, Nebuchadrezzar II, gained control of Syria and Palestine in swift campaigns. The defeated Egyptians, however, continued to intrigue in Palestine, whose native states repeatedly joined anti-Babylonian coalitions, all of which collapsed of themselves or were crushed by the Chaldean armies. Jerusalem was twice besieged, in 597 and after 589. Finally, about 587/586, it was stormed and destroyed. The prophet Jeremiah, who had foreseen the tragic denouement and had repeatedly warned his people against their suicidal policy, died in Egypt. Judah was devastated and almost depopulated.

The Persian empire

In 539 bce Cyrus II of the Persian Achaemenian dynasty followed up his triumph over Media by conquering Lydia and Babylonia, thus making himself ruler of the greatest empire thitherto known. In the administrative reforms implemented by Darius I (reigned 522–486 bce), Phoenicia, Palestine-Syria, and Cyprus constituted the fifth province (satrapy) of the Persian empire (Herodotus, The History, Book III, chapter 91).

One of Cyrus's first acts was to decree (c. 538 bce) that Judah be restored and the Temple of Jerusalem be rebuilt. A large number of Jewish exiles in Babylonia returned to Jerusalem, and work on the Second Temple was begun. The political situation was extremely unfavourable, however, since Judah south of Hebron had been occupied by Edomites escaping from Arab pressure, while the tiny remainder north of Hebron had passed under the control of the governor of Samaria. In spite of political intrigues to prevent completion of the work of rebuilding the Temple, the Jews took advantage of the civil wars and rebellions that racked the empire after the accession of Darius I to press forward with the work. They were urged on by the fiery prophets Haggai and Zechariah. In 515 bce the Second Temple was finished, but the Jews had meanwhile aroused the suspicion of the Persian authorities, and further efforts to improve their situation were discouraged.

Matters rested in this unsatisfactory state until about 445 bce, when the Jewish royal favourite, Nehemiah, deeply stirred by reports of the sorry condition of Judah and Jerusalem, succeeded in obtaining the Persian ruler's support for a mission to Palestine. Under Nehemiah's leadership, Jerusalem's walls were rebuilt. Knowledge of the exact sequence of events is complicated by the confused state of the documentary sources, and the chronology of events in the time of Nehemiah and Ezra, who became a leader of the Jews who had returned to Jerusalem from Babylonia, is not certain.

There is good evidence to suggest that Ezra's return to Jerusalem should be dated to 398 bce, early in the reign of the Persian king Artaxerxes II. The mention of

Persian intervention in the priestly affairs of the high priest Johanan can reasonably be associated with Ezra's reform activities. In any event, Nehemiah and Ezra were able to establish both the religious autonomy of Judah and the practice of normative Judaism so firmly that they continued with little change for several centuries.

Information concerning the history of Palestine in the period following the age of Nehemiah and Ezra is scanty. It is known that the province of Judah continued to be administered by high priests who struck their own coins and that the provinces of Samaria and Ammon remained under governors of the houses of Sanballat and Tobiah. In 343 Artaxerxes III (Ochus) is said to have devastated parts of Palestine in connection with his reconquest of Egypt. Eleven years later the country passed into Macedonian hands after Alexander the Great's conquest of Phoenicia.

From Alexander the Great to 70 ce

To Alexander, Palestine was, as to many before him, a corridor leading to Egypt, the outlying Persian province. Consequently, in his attack on that province after the Battle of Issus (333 bce), he confined his attention, in his passage southward, to reducing the coastal cities that might form bases for the Persian fleet. He left the Jews undisturbed in their religion and customs. The high priest remained the head of the Jewish state, perhaps assisted by a council of elders. (See ancient Greek civilization: Alexander the Great and Hellenistic Age.)

The Ptolemies

After the death of Alexander in 323 bce, Palestine, with much of Syria and Phoenicia, fell to Ptolemy I (Soter), who established himself as satrap in Egypt that same year and adopted the title of king by 304. (After the death of Ptolemy, the Ptolemaic dynasty ruled Egypt for 300 years.)

The successors of Alexander, including Ptolemy and Seleucus I (Nicator), defeated Antigonus I (Monophthalmus), another of Alexander's generals, who had almost succeeded in re-creating under his sole rule Alexander's vast empire, at the Battle of Ipsus in Phrygia in 301 bce. This victory confirmed Ptolemy in his possession of his territory, although he had arrived too late for the battle, and Seleucus, whose participation in it had been decisive, at first disputed Ptolemy's claim to Syria and Phoenicia and actually occupied northern Syria. This early dispute laid the foundations of a century of bitter antagonism between the houses of Ptolemy and Seleucus that led to war five times the so-called Syrian Wars and was finally stilled only when Palestine, in 200 bce, became part of the Seleucid kingdom. The northern boundary of the kingdom established by Ptolemy lay apparently slightly north of modern Tripoli, Lebanon, perhaps on the course of the Kabīr River (ancient Eleutherus), and there are no signs of any important change in this frontier throughout the next century.

Of Ptolemaic rule in the southern part of this territory, Palestine, little is known. The small amount of information there is mainly from writers of a later period, especially the author of the First Book of Maccabees and the Jewish historian Flavius Josephus suggests that, unlike the northern region, known as Syria and Phoenicia, the area was left in much its previous state, with considerable power and authority in the hands of the native chieftains.

More is known of taxation than of administration. A story preserved by Josephus (The Antiquities of the Jews, Book XII, section 154 ff.) indicates that tax farming, whereby the right to collect taxes was auctioned or was awarded to privileged persons, was employed for the collection of local taxes. It seems likely that there were additional extraordinary taxes levied by edict from Egypt.

Knowledge of the economic and commercial life of Palestine in the mid-3rd century bce is, on the other hand, fuller and more reliable. It is drawn from the dossier of letters received and written by one Zenon, the confidential business manager of the chief minister of Ptolemy II (Philadelphus; 285–246 bce). In 259 Zenon was sent to Palestine and Syria, where his master had commercial interests.

His letters speak particularly of a trade in slaves, especially of young girls for prostitution, in whom there appears to have been a brisk commerce, with export to Egypt. Zenon's records also testify to a considerable trade in cereals, oil, and wine. Inevitably, like all imports to Egypt, Palestinian exports worked under state monopoly, without which the internal monopolies of Egypt would have been undermined. Palestine, like Egypt and Syria, seems to have had no economic freedom under Ptolemaic rule; in all transactions the hand of the government's agents is clearly visible.

Far less is known of the material culture of Palestine in the Ptolemaic period. The population seems, as in Syria, to have been divided between the Hellenized cities (poleis) of the coast, notably Ascalon (modern Ashqelon, Israel) and Joppa (modern Tel Aviv–Yafo), and the rural population living in villages (komai). The fact that several cities had Ptolemaic dynastic names (Philadelphia, Philoteria, Ptolemais) must not lead to the conclusion that the early Ptolemies wanted to urbanize and raise the standard of living of the people of Palestine. It seldom appears that they did more than rename a previously existing city (e.g., Scythopolis for Bet She'an) a practice not uncommon in the Hellenistic world. In fact, unlike the Seleucids, the Ptolemies do not appear to have been great city builders. Nor do they appear to have encouraged the outward forms of independence in local government. It seems likely from the story of the Phoenician tax farmers mentioned above that considerable authority lay in the hands of the wealthy; yet the fact that both Ascalon and Joppa issued Ptolemaic regal coinage, but apparently no autonomous bronze coinage, suggests a rigid control.

The absence of epigraphic evidence from the cities of Ptolemaic Palestine, however, renders any judgment about the conditions of the cities hazardous. Archaeology, too, helps but little, inasmuch as the buildings of Roman Palestine superseded most of the Hellenistic remains. One exception must be noted: the tombs of the Hellenized Sidonian military settlers at Marisa in Edom (Idumaea) the walls of which are decorated with frescoes of fine hunting scenes indicate that Hellenic civilization had been embraced by the non-Greek population in that period.

The chronic state of hostility between Ptolemaic Egypt and the Seleucid house, which in much of the 3rd century bce had been concerned with the coastal regions of western Asia Minor, received a new impetus with the accession to the Seleucid throne of the energetic Antiochus III (the Great; 223–187), who aimed to win southern Syria and Palestine from Egypt, now weakly governed, and thereby establish the frontier to which Seleucus I had unwillingly renounced his claim in 301 bce.

After his decisive defeat by Ptolemy IV (Philopator) at Raphia in 217, however, Antiochus was for several years occupied with internal troubles, and it was therefore not until about 200 bce that he could think again of an attack on Egypt. There a child Ptolemy V (Epiphanes) had recently ascended the throne, and the government was in the hands of overly powerful ministers who were more concerned with enriching themselves than with preserving the integrity of the kingdom. At Panion, on the northern boundary of Galilee, the armies of Antiochus and Ptolemy met, and Ptolemy was defeated. Thus the Ptolemaic possessions north of the Sinai desert, including Palestine, passed into the hands of the house of Seleucus.

The Seleucids

The Seleucids brought to the problem of the administration of Palestine a different tradition from that which had been behind Ptolemaic rule. The latter was based on the careful exploitation of territory that was possible in a small and closely knit land such as Egypt and had thence been extended to the Ptolemaic provinces. This had never been possible for the Seleucids, who had always been masters of regions so vast as to render a unified and absolute control impossible. There is no sign that the Seleucid government oppressed the native peoples they seem, on the contrary, to have aimed at improving the natives' status as far as possible, largely through bringing them into contact with Greek modes of urban existence.

It might then be supposed that Seleucid rule would have been popular in Palestine. In fact, however, it was under Seleucid rule that the great uprising of the Jewish people, the revolt of the Maccabees, occurred. The explanation of this paradox is perhaps twofold. First, the Seleucids were in need of money, and, second, the throne, at a critical time, was occupied by a tactless and neurotic king. Knowledge of Seleucid rule in Palestine before the accession of Antiochus IV (Epiphanes; 175–164 bce) is slight.

The period from 188 bce onward was a lean time for the dynasty, because the war with Rome, which had ended (in 189) in a complete Roman victory, had cost it not only almost the whole of Asia Minor (Anatolia) but also a yearly indemnity of 15,000 talents. It is therefore not surprising that the first glimpse of Seleucid rule in Palestine tells of an attempt by Heliodorus, the leading minister of Seleucus IV (Philopator; 187–175 bce), to deprive the Second Temple in Jerusalem of its treasure. His failure was soon ascribed to divine protection.

With the accession of Antiochus Epiphanes, relations rapidly deteriorated. Antiochus appears to have aimed at a wholesale restoration of the Seleucid empire in the east, including an occupation of Egypt, as a counter to the loss of the western province occasioned by the Treaty of Apamea. He made an unwise beginning in Palestine by establishing a philhellene high priest, and it is clear from this and from his whole subsequent policy that he wished to extirpate Jewish religion from its central stronghold (there is no indication that he persecuted Jews of the Diaspora [Greek: "Dispersion"] living in the cities of his kingdom).

Antiochus invaded Egypt in 170 or 169 bce, returning to Syria by way of Jerusalem, where he and his army despoiled the Temple of all its wealth. Two years later, after his humiliating expulsion from the gate of Egypt by the Roman legate, he sent a financial official to exact taxes from the cities of Judaea. Antiochus's official attacked the city of Jerusalem by guile and largely destroyed it.

He then built a fortified position on the citadel, called by the Greeks the Akra. This became the symbol of Judah's enslavement, though in itself the presence of a royal garrison in a Hellenistic city was by no means unusual. Its imposition was followed by an open attack on religious practice, in which many rites were forbidden. Noncompliance with the order which contained many items calculated to raise the bitterest resistance in the hearts of law-abiding Jews, such as the prohibition of circumcision and the abolition of the observance of the Sabbath was punishable by death.

Finally, on the 25th day of the Hebrew month Kislev (December) in 168 bce, the "abomination of desolation," namely the altar of Zeus, was set up in the Temple in Jerusalem. It was this above all that summoned forth the resistance of the sons of the aged priest Mattathias; thus began the Maccabean revolt, led by Judas Maccabeus.

The resistance, it must be emphasized, came from only a section of the population. The century and a half of Greek rule had Hellenized much of the upper class of Jerusalem, and some of the characteristic features of Greek city life such as the ephebic institute, for the training of young men, and the gymnasia had been established on the initiative of this section of the ruling class, which was able to accept a less radical observance of Judaism and combine it with loyalty to the throne. Throughout the revolt, and indeed until the closing days of the Hasmonean dynasty established by the Maccabeans, this Hellenized element had to be taken into account.

Judas Maccabeus proved himself a leader of high quality. He successfully resisted the weak forces sent by the Seleucid authorities, and after three years of intermittent warfare he succeeded in purifying the Temple (165 bce). The Akra, however, remained in Seleucid hands until 141 bce.

After the death of Antiochus Epiphanes in 164 bce, the numbers of claimants to the Seleucid throne made a continuous policy toward Palestine impossible, because each claimant felt the need to seek support wherever it might be found. Thus, Jewish high priests were bribed by the kings and dynasts of Syria. This development enabled Judas and those who succeeded him to hold their own and eventually to establish a hereditary dynasty, known as the Hasmonean for their ancestor Hasmoneus.

Soon after Antiochus Epiphanes' death, an agreement was reached with the Seleucid regent Lysias (who feared the appearance of a rival in Syria) through which the Jews received back their religious liberty. But, at the same time, the regular practice of pagan worship, beside the Jewish, was established, and a Seleucid nominee was appointed high priest. Thus were laid the seeds of fresh revolt.

Almost immediately Judas again took the field and scored a considerable victory over Nicanor, the Seleucid general, in which the latter was killed. Within two months, however, Demetrius I (Soter), the Seleucid king, sent Bacchides to take up a position near Jerusalem, and, in the engagement that followed, Judas lost his life (161/160 bce).

The Hasmonean priest-princes

In the following years, dynastic disputes within the Seleucid empire prevented a succession of rulers from settling the Palestinian question. These circumstances allowed first Jonathan (161/160–143/142 bce), the brother and successor of Judas, and then his brother Simon (143/142–134) to attain power. In 153 one of the Seleucid pretenders, Alexander Balas, in order to outplay the legitimate king, Demetrius, granted Jonathan the office of high priest and gave him the Seleucid rank of a courtier, thereby legitimizing his position.

When Simon succeeded Jonathan, he acquired the status of a recognized secular ruler; the year he assumed rule was regarded as the first of a new era, and official documents were dated in his name and by his regnal year. He secured from the new Seleucid monarch, Demetrius II (Nicator; 145–139 and 129–125), exemption from taxation for the Jews.

In 142–141 bce Simon forced the Syrian garrison on the Akra to surrender, and the Jews passed a decree in his honour, granting the right of permanent incumbency to Simon and to his successors, until "an accredited prophet" should arise. It was thus in Simon's reign that the rule of the priest-prince was transformed into a secular hereditary rule. The Seleucid king recognized this, granting Simon the right to issue his own coins.

Simon's son, John Hyrcanus I (134–104 bce), suffered an initial setback at the hands of the last great Seleucid king, Antiochus VII (Sidetes), who set out to reconquer Palestine, but at the latter's death John renewed his father's expansionist program, in which Samaria was conquered and destroyed. In internal policy, however, he committed the grave error of quarreling with one of the two main Jewish ecclesiastical parties, the Pharisees who followed the Law with great strictness and with whom the Maccabean movement had in origin close affinity and siding with their opponents, the more liberal Sadducees.

This is an early instance of that denial of the revolutionary origin of the movement that became entirely obvious in the reign of Alexander Jannaeus. Hyrcanus I was succeeded by Aristobulus I (104–103), who extended Hasmonean territory northward and is said to have assumed the title of king (basileus), though on his coins he appears, like Hyrcanus I, as high priest.

The reign of his brother and successor, Alexander Jannaeus, was long (103–76 bce) and largely filled with wars. Alexander imposed his rule rigorously over an increasingly large area, including both the cities of the coast and the area east of the Jordan River. Still more clearly than Hyrcanus I, he attests the change in direction and aim of the Hasmonean house. He was the bitter enemy of the Pharisees, his coins bear Greek as well as Hebrew legends, and his title on them is simply "King Alexander."

He was succeeded by his widow, Salome Alexandra, who reversed his policy and was guided by powerful religious advisers, members of the Pharisaic movement. After her death in 67 bce her two sons Aristobulus II and Hyrcanus II fought for the succession. Hyrcanus was defeated but was encouraged to reassert his rights by Antipater, an Edomite, son of the governor of Idumaea and father of the future Herod the Great.

At that stage the Romans appeared on the scene. Pompey the Great, during his reorganization of the lands of the newly conquered Seleucid kingdom, also arranged the affairs of Palestine (63 bce). He attempted to arbitrate between the brothers and eventually, after he had laid siege to and captured Jerusalem, appointed Hyrcanus II as high priest without the title of king adopted by his predecessors.

He also imposed taxes on the Jews and curtailed Jewish dominions, granting virtual autonomy to a group of 10 or 11 Hellenized cities in Syria and Palestine, thenceforth to be known as the Decapolis, and placing them under the jurisdiction of the newly appointed governor of Syria. Pliny the Elder lists these cities as Damascus, Philadelphia (modern Amman, Jordan), Raphana, Scythopolis, Gadara, Hippos, Dion, Pella, Gerasa, and Canatha. On the basis of evidence in inscriptions, Abila can be added to the list.

Thus, despite the name Decapolis, the actual number appears to have been 11. All these cities, except Scythopolis, are located east of the Jordan River, extending from Damascus in the north to Philadelphia in the south. Except for Damascus, all the other cities lie immediately to the east of Galilee, Samaria, or Judaea.

Whether the Decapolis geographically belonged to Syria, to Coele Syria ("Hollow Syria"; i.e., the southernmost region of Syria, which may include Palestine and is sometimes mistakenly limited to the modern Al-Biqāʿ valley), or to Arabia (often identified as the land east of the Jordan River) is not clear, especially in the ancient geographers. In any event, the Decapolis ended as a political entity when Rome annexed Arabia in 106 ce; the cities were distributed among the three provinces of Arabia, Judaea, and Syria. It appears that Philadelphia, Gerasa, and probably Dion went to Arabia, Damascus certainly to Syria, and the rest to Judaea or Syria.

After the death of Pompey, however, the power of Antipater and his family greatly increased. Hyrcanus II became a figurehead of no importance, and Antipater himself, in return for services to Julius Caesar, received Roman citizenship and was awarded the title of "procurator of Judaea," while his sons Phasael and

Herod became governors (strategoi) of Jerusalem and Galilee, respectively. The unexpected occupation of Palestine by Parthian troops in 40 bce altered the situation. Antigonus, the son of Aristobulus and therefore a legitimate Hasmonean, won the favour of the Parthians and was established by them as king and high priest of Jerusalem. Phasael was reported to have committed suicide, while his brother Herod escaped to Rome.

The Herodian house and the Roman procurators

Herod, in Rome, was recognized by the Senate, with the approval of Octavian (later the emperor Caesar Augustus) and Mark Antony, as king of Judaea (40 bce) and returned to Palestine in 39. Shortly afterward Roman troops expelled the Parthians, whose popularity in Palestine had been and subsequently remained considerable.

After struggles against Antigonus, the Parthian nominee, in which he was assisted by Roman troops, Herod eventually captured Jerusalem. At about the same time, he married a niece of Antigonus, thus probably consoling those who remained loyal to the memory of the almost defunct Hasmonean house. Antigonus, when he fell into the hands of his enemies, was executed by order of Mark Antony.

The accession of Herod, a Roman protégé and an Edomite, brought to Palestine the peace that in the years of independence it had often lacked. His long reign (37–4 bce) was marked by general prosperity; his new city of Caesarea (Caesarea Maritima) received lavish praise from Josephus for its spectacular port and extensive water and sewer system. Between 31 and 20, Augustus restored to him the Jewish territories that Pompey had taken away, and in this enlarged kingdom he created a sound administrative system of Hellenistic type.

Toward the end of his life the complex demands of a vast family (he had at least nine wives) led him into difficulties regarding the succession, and it was then that he developed into the gruesome and vicious figure that Christian tradition has made so familiar. He had his wife Mariamne and several of his sons put to death to prevent them from succeeding him; and on his death in 4 bce the country again entered a period of divided rule, which led to the reestablishment of direct Roman government.

Augustus decided later that year, in the presence of three surviving sons of Herod, that Herod Archelaus should rule Judaea, Samaria, and Edom (i.e., central and southern Palestine); Herod Antipas should rule Galilee and Peraea (east of the Jordan River); and Philip should rule Trachonitis, Batanaea, and Auranitis (the area between the Decapolis and Damascus).

The fates of these rulers (of whom Philip and Antipas were called tetrarchs, Archelaus ethnarch) and their territories were different. Philip, the most peaceable of the three, ruled the northern area until his death in 34 ce. Antipas reigned in Galilee and Peraea until 39 ce but was then banished by the emperor Caligula on the ground that he had parleyed with Rome's enemies. Archelaus reigned for 10 years only; he was removed at the request of his subjects in 6 ce.

The region under Archelaus's rule (i.e., Judaea, Samaria, and Edom) became the province of Judaea and passed to a series of undistinguished Roman prefects, the last of whom (Pontius Pilate, 26–36 ce) lost office for the unnecessary massacre of some Samaritans. Palestine finally was united under Caligula's protégé, Herod Agrippa I, who succeeded Philip in the north in 37 ce.

The tetrarchy of Antipas was added soon after his removal in 39, and the territories of Judaea, Samaria, and Edom were added in 41, so that from 41 to his death in 44 Agrippa ruled the kingdom of his grandfather, Herod the Great, from Jerusalem. In 44 the entire kingdom passed under Roman rule and was reconstituted as the procuratorial province of Judaea.

Disturbances in the early years of procuratorial rule were frequent and caused largely by maladministration. Serious trouble arose under Ventidius Cumanus (48–52); and under his successor, the imperial freedman Felix (52–60), rebellion was open though sporadic. The incompetence and anti-Jewish posture of Gessius Florus, procurator 64–66, led in 66 to the decisive and final outbreak, known as the First Jewish Revolt.

Florus, the heir to a long tradition of hostility between the large Hellenized populations of Palestine and the

Jews (also a problem in the Diaspora, most notably at Alexandria during the reign of Caligula), allowed the Greek population of Caesarea Maritima to massacre the Jews of that city with impunity. Greeks in other towns of Palestine repeated the assault. In turn, the Jews responded by slaughtering Gentiles in Samaria, Galilee, and elsewhere. Soon Florus lost control of the situation. The organization of the Jews was better than it previously had been, and they were successful in an early engagement against the governor of Syria, who had advanced to Palestine with two legions to assist the hard-pressed procurator.

In 67, however, Vespasian, the future emperor, with his son Titus, arrived with a force of about 60,000 men, and the war became increasingly bitter. By the end of 67 Galilee was captured, and Judaea was reduced in three campaigns, which ended with the fall of Jerusalem in 70. The Temple was destroyed, though tradition recorded that Titus gave orders that it was to be spared, and the city became the permanent garrison town of a Roman legion. By 73 all resistance had ceased.

Events in Palestine during the first decades of the Christian era were of crucial importance to the development of Christianity as a world religion and to the re-creation of Judaism as a Diaspora community and the eventual establishment of Rabbinic Judaism as the normative expression of Jewish religious and cultural life. For a discussion of the founding of Christianity, see Jesus Christ, Christianity, and biblical literature; for the subsequent history of Judaism following the dispersion, see Judaism and Diaspora.

Roman Palestine

After the destruction of Jerusalem, a legion (X Fretensis) was stationed on the site, and the rank of the provincial governor was raised from procurator to legatus Augusti, signifying a change from equestrian to senatorial rank. Caesarea Maritima, the governor's residence, became a Roman colony, and, as a reward for the loyalty of the Greeks in the revolt, a new pagan city, Neapolis (modern Nābulus in the West Bank), was founded at Shechem, the religious centre of the Samaritans.

The Jews, deprived of the Temple, founded a new religious centre in the rabbinical school of Jamnia (Jabneh). When a revolt broke out in 115 ce, the Roman emperor Trajan appointed the first consular legate of Judaea, Lucius Quietus, to suppress it. The rank of the legate confirms that two legions were stationed in Judaea, one at Jerusalem, the other at Caparcotna in Galilee, and thenceforth the province must have held consular status.

In 132 the emperor Hadrian decided to build a Roman colony, Aelia Capitolina, on the site of Jerusalem. The announcement of his plan, as well as his ban on circumcision (revoked later, but only for the Jews), provoked a much more serious uprising, the Second Jewish Revolt, led by Bar Kokhba.

It was ruthlessly repressed by Julius Severus; according to certain accounts, almost 1,000 villages were destroyed and more than half a million people killed. In Judaea proper the Jews seem to have been virtually exterminated, but they survived in Galilee, which, like Samaria, appears to have held aloof from the revolt. Tiberias in Galilee became the seat of the Jewish patriarchs.

The province of Judaea was renamed Syria Palaestina (later simply called Palaestina), and, according to Eusebius of Caeseria (Ecclesiastical History, Book IV, chapter 6), no Jew was thenceforth allowed to set foot in Jerusalem or the surrounding district. This prohibition apparently was relaxed sometime later to permit Jews to enter Jerusalem one day a year, on a day of mourning called Tisha be-Ava.

Although this ban was officially still in force as late as the 4th century ce, there is some evidence that from the Severan period onward (after 193) Jews visited the city more frequently, especially at certain festival times, and even that there may have been some Jews in residence. About the time the Bar Kokhba revolt was crushed (135), Hadrian proceeded to convert Jerusalem into a Greco-Roman city, with a circus, an amphitheatre, baths, and a theatre and with streets conforming to the Roman grid pattern.

He also erected temples dedicated to Jupiter and himself (Aelia was his clan name) on the very site of the destroyed Temple of Jerusalem. To repopulate the city, Hadrian apparently brought in Greco-Syrians from the surrounding areas and even perhaps some legionary veterans. The urbanization and Hellenization of Palestine was continued during the reign of the emperor Septimius Severus (193–211 ce), except in Galilee, where the Jewish presence remained strong. New pagan cities were founded in Judaea at Eleutheropolis and Diospolis (formerly Lydda) and at Nicopolis (formerly Emmaus) under one of Severus's successors, Elagabalus (218–222).

In addition, Severus issued a specific ban against Jewish proselytism.

After Constantine I converted to Christianity early in the 4th century, a new era of prosperity began for Palestine. The emperor himself built a magnificent church on the site of the Holy Sepulchre, the most sacred of Christian holy places; his mother, Saint Helena, built two others at the place of the Nativity at Bethlehem and of the Ascension in Jerusalem and his mother-in-law, Eutropia, built a church at Mamre.

Palestine began to attract floods of pilgrims from all parts of the empire.

It also became a great centre of the eremitic life (idiorrhythmic monasticism); men flocked from all quarters to become hermits in the Judaean wilderness, which was soon dotted with monasteries. Constantine added the southern half of Arabia to the province, but in 357–358 (or perhaps as late as the 390s) the addition was made a separate province under the name of Palaestina or Salutaris (later Palaestina Tertia).

At the end of the 4th century, an enlarged Palestine was divided into three provinces: Prima, with its capital at Caesarea; Secunda, with its capital at Scythopolis (Bet She'an); and Salutaris, with its capital at Petra or possibly for a time at Elusa. It is clear that the province of Palaestina underwent several territorial changes in the 4th century ce, but the details and the chronology remain obscure. The governor of Prima bore the high rank of proconsul from 382 to 385 and again as part of East Rome, which came to be known as the Byzantine Empire after 476 from 535 onward. A dux of Palestine commanded the garrison of all three provinces.

The bishop of the civil capital, Caesarea, was, according to the usual rule, metropolitan of the province, but the bishops of Jerusalem were claiming special prerogatives as early as the first Council of Nicaea (325). Eventually, Juvenal, bishop of Jerusalem from 421 to 458, achieved his ambition and was recognized by the Council of Chalcedon (451) as patriarch of the three provinces of Palestine.

There was a revolt of the Jews in Galilee in 352, which was suppressed by Gallus Caesar. Under Marcian (450–457) and again under the Byzantine emperor Justinian I (527–565), the Samaritans revolted. Palestine, like Syria and Egypt, was also troubled by the Monophysite controversy, a debate among Christians who disagreed with the Council of Chalcedon's assertion that the person of Jesus Christ comprised two natures, human and divine.

When Juvenal returned from Chalcedon, having signed the Council's canons, the monks of Palestine rose and elected another bishop of Jerusalem, and military force was required to subdue them. Gradually, however, the Chalcedonian doctrine gained ground, and Palestine became a stronghold of orthodoxy.

Apart from these disturbances, the country enjoyed peace and prosperity until 611, when Khosrow II, king of Persia, launched an invasion of Byzantine territory. His troops captured Jerusalem (614), destroyed churches, and carried off the True Cross. In 628 the Byzantine emperor Heraclius recovered Palestine, and he subsequently restored the True Cross to Jerusalem, but 10 years later Arab armies invaded both the Persian and the Byzantine empires.

From the Arab conquest to 1900

The rise of Islam

The successful unification of the Arabian Peninsula under Islam by the first caliph, Abū Bakr (632–634), made it possible to channel the expansion of the Arab Muslims into new directions. Abū Bakr, therefore, summoned the faithful to a holy war (jihad) and quickly amassed a large army. He dispatched three detachments of about 3,000 (later increased to about 7,500) men each to start operations in southern and southeastern Syria. He died, however, before he could witness the results of these undertakings. The conquests he started were carried on by his successor, the caliph 'Umar I (634–644).

The first battle took place at Wadi Al-'Arabah, south of the Dead Sea. The Byzantine defenders were defeated and retreated toward Gaza but were overtaken and almost annihilated. In other places, however, the natural advantages of the defenders were more effective, and the invaders were hard-pressed. Khālid ibn al-Walīd, then operating in southern Iraq, was ordered to the aid of his fellow Arab generals on the Syrian front, and the combined forces won a bloody victory on July 30, 634, at a place in southern Palestine that the sources call Ajnādayn. All of Palestine then lay open to the invaders.

In the meantime, the emperor Heraclius was mustering his own large army and in 636 dispatched it against the Muslims. Khālid concentrated his troops on the Yarmūk River, the eastern tributary of the Jordan River. The decisive battle that delivered Palestine to the Muslims took place on August 20, 636. Only Jerusalem and Caesarea held out, the former until 638, when it surrendered to the Muslims, and the latter until October 640. Palestine, and indeed all of Syria, was then in Muslim hands.

After the surrender of Jerusalem, 'Umar divided Palestine into two administrative districts (jund) similar to the Roman and Byzantine provinces: they were Jordan (Al-'Urdūn) and Palestine (Filasṭīn). Jordan included Galilee and Acre (modern 'Akko, Israel) and extended east to the desert; Palestine, with its capital first at Lydda (modern Lod, Israel) and later at Ramla (after 716), covered the region south of the Plain of Esdraelon.

'Umar lost no time in emphasizing Islam's interest in the holy city of Jerusalem as the first qiblah toward which, until 623, Muslims had turned their faces in prayer and as the third holiest spot in Islam. (The Prophet Muhammad himself had changed the qiblah to Mecca in 623.) On visiting the Temple Mount area which Muslims came to know as Al-Ḥaram al-Sharīf (Arabic: "The Noble Sanctuary") and finding the place suffering from neglect, 'Umar and his followers cleaned it with their own hands and declared it a sacred place of prayer, erecting there the first structure called Al-Aqṣā Mosque.

Under the Umayyads, a Muslim dynasty that gained power in 661 from the Meccans and Medinans who had initially led the Islamic community, Palestine formed, with Syria, one of the main provinces of the empire. Each jund was administered by an emir assisted by a financial officer. This pattern continued, in general, until the time of Ottoman rule.

For various reasons, the Umayyads paid special attention to Palestine. The process of Arabization and Islamization was gaining momentum there. It was one of the mainstays of Umayyad power and was important in their struggle against both Iraq and the Arabian Peninsula. The caliph ʿAbd al-Malik ibn Marwān (685–705) erected the Dome of the Rock in 691 on the site of the Temple of Solomon, which the Muslims believed had been the halting station of the

Prophet on his nocturnal journey to heaven. (See isrā' and mi'rāj.)

This magnificent structure represents the earliest Muslim monument still extant. Close to the shrine and to the south, 'Abd al-Malik's son, al-Walīd I (705–715), rebuilt Al-Aqṣa Mosque on a larger scale. The Umayyad caliph 'Umar II (717–720) imposed humiliating restrictions on his non-Muslim subjects, particularly the Christians. Conversions arising from convenience as well as conviction then increased.

These conversions to Islam, together with a steady tribal inflow from the desert, changed the religious character of Palestine's inhabitants. The predominantly Christian population gradually became predominantly Muslim and Arabic-speaking. At the same time, during the early years of Muslim control of the city, a small permanent Jewish population returned to Jerusalem after a 500-year absence.

ʿAbbāsid rule

Umayyad rule ended in 750. Along with Syria, Palestine became subject to ʿAbbāsid authority, based in Baghdad, and, like Syria, it did not readily submit to its new masters. Unlike the Umayyads, who leaned on the Yemeni (South Arabian) tribes, the ʿAbbāsids, in Syria, favoured and indeed used the Qays (North Arabian) tribes. Enmity between the two groups was, therefore, intensified and became an important political factor in Palestine.

Pro-Umayyad uprisings were frequent and received Palestinian support. In 840/841 Abū Ḥarb, a Yemenite, unfurled the white banner of the Umayyads and succeeded in recruiting a large number of peasant followers, mainly among the Palestinian population, who regarded him as the saviour whose appearance was to save the land from the hated ʿAbbāsids. Though the insurrection was put down, unrest persisted.

The process of Islamization gained momentum under the ʿAbbāsids. ʿAbbāsid rulers encouraged the settlement and fortification of coastal Palestine so as to secure it against the Byzantine enemy. During the second half of the 9th century, however, signs of internal decay began to appear in the ʿAbbāsid empire. Petty states, and some indeed not so petty, emerged in different parts of the realm.

One of the first to affect Palestine was the Tūlūnid dynasty (868–905) of Egypt, which marked the beginning of the disengagement of Egypt and, with it, of Syria and Palestine from ʿAbbāsid rule. During that period Palestine also experienced the destructive operations of the Qarmaṭians, an Ismāʿīlī Shīʿite sect that launched an insurrection in 903–906. After ʿAbbāsid authority was briefly restored, Palestine came under Ikhshīdid rule (935–969).

The Fāṭimid dynasty

In the meantime, the Shī'ite Fāṭimid dynasty was rising to power in North Africa. It moved eastward to seize not only Egypt but also Palestine and Syria and to threaten Baghdad itself. The Fāṭimids seized Egypt from the Ikhshīdids in 969 and in less than a decade were able to establish a precarious control over Palestine, where they faced Qarmaṭian, Seljuq, Byzantine, and periodic Bedouin opposition. Palestine was thus often reduced to a battlefield. The country suffered even greater hardship, however, under the Fāṭimid caliph al-Ḥākim (996–1021),

whose behaviour was at times erratic and extremely harsh, particularly toward his non-Muslim subjects. He reactivated earlier discriminatory laws imposed on Christians and Jews and added new ones. In 1009 he ordered the destruction of the Church of the Holy Sepulchre, which was severely damaged as a result.

In 1071 the Seljuqs captured Jerusalem, which prospered as pilgrimages by Jews, Christians, and Muslims increased despite political instability. The Fāṭimids recaptured the city in 1098 only to relinquish it a year later to a new enemy, the Crusaders of western Europe.

The Crusades

A year after the capture of Jerusalem by the Crusaders, the Latin kingdom of Jerusalem was established (Christmas Day, 1100). Thereafter there was no effective check to the expansion of the Crusaders' power until the capture of their stronghold at Edessa (modern Şanlıurfa, Turkey) by the atabeg (governor) of Mosul, ʿImād al-Dīn Zangī ibn Aq Sonqur, in 1144. Zangī's anti-Crusader campaign was carried on after his death by his son Nūr al-Dīn Maḥmūd (Nureddin) and, more effectively, by the sultan Ṣalāh al-Dīn Yūsuf ibn

Ayyūb (commonly known in the West as Saladin), a protégé of the atabeg's family.

After consolidating his position in Egypt and Syria, Saladin waged relentless war against the "infidel" Franks (Western Christians). On July 4, 1187, six days after the capture of Tiberias, he dealt the Crusaders a crushing blow at the decisive Battle of Ḥaṭṭīn (Ḥiṭṭīn). Most of Palestine was once again Muslim.

Further attempts by the Crusaders to regain control of Palestine proved ineffective, primarily because of incessant quarrels among the Crusaders themselves. Ironically, it was left to an emperor of dubious Christian standing, Frederick II, to negotiate in 1229, while under excommunication, a 10-year treaty that temporarily restored Jerusalem, Nazareth, and Bethlehem to the Christians. In 1244, however, the Ayyūbid sultan al-Ṣāliḥ Ayyūb definitively restored Jerusalem to Islam.

While the Ayyūbids of Saladin's house were losing ground to the Turkish-speaking Mamlūks in Egypt, the Mongol sweep westward continued, placing the Crusaders, as it were, between two fires. To make matters worse, the Crusaders themselves were hopelessly riddled with dissension. In 1260 the Mamlūk leader Baybars I emerged as a champion of Muslim resurgence. After taking part in the defeat of the Mongols at the Battle of ʿAyn Jālūt in Palestine, he murdered the incumbent sultan and seized the throne; in the years 1263 to 1271 he carried out annual raids against the harassed Franks. His efforts were continued by the sultan al-Ashraf Ṣalāḥ al-Dīn Khalīl, during whose reign the last of the Crusaders were driven out of Acre (May 18, 1291). A chapter in the history of Palestine thus came to an end. The Mamlūks and subsequent Muslim regimes ruled the area with only brief interruptions for the next 600 years.

Palestine under the Mamlūks in the 14th century saw a period of prosperity for some; this was especially notable in Jerusalem, where the government sponsored an elaborate program to construct schools, establish lodgings for travelers and Muslim pilgrims, and renovate mosques. Tax revenues, collected mainly from the villages, were spent largely on support of religious institutions. Palestine formed a part of the district of Damascus, second only to Egypt in the Mamlūk domains.

The region suffered the ravages of several epidemics, including the great pestilence, the same Black Death that in 1347–51 devastated Europe. The fall of the Baḥrī Mamlūks and the rise of the Burjī Mamlūks (1382–1517) contributed to a gradual economic deterioration and a decrease in security. During the reigns of the second Burjī sultan, Faraj (1399–1405 and 1405–12), the last onslaught of the Mongols, which made the name of Timur (Tamerlane) a synonym of destruction and plunder, took place.

Although Palestine was spared the pillage of his hordes, it could not escape its disastrous repercussions as the Mamlūks moved through in a vain attempt to defend Damascus against the invader. The death of Timur in 1405, and the weakness of Iran in the ensuing century, pitted the Mamlūks against the rising power of the Ottoman Empire for the control of western Asia. Hostilities broke out in 1486 when Sultan Qā'it Bāy contested with Bayezid II the possession of some border towns. The climax came three decades later on August 24, 1516, when the Ottoman sultan, Selim I, routed the Mamlūk armies at the Battle of Marj Dābiq. Palestine began its four centuries under Ottoman domination.

Ottoman rule

Under the Ottoman Turks, Palestine continued to be linked administratively to Damascus until 1830, when it was placed under Sidon, then under Acre, then once again under Damascus until 1887–88, at which time the administrative divisions of the Ottoman Empire were settled for the last time. Palestine was divided into the districts of Nāblus and Acre, both of which were linked with the province of Beirut and the autonomous district of Jerusalem, which dealt directly with Istanbul.

With varying fortunes often accompanied by revolts, massacres, and wars, the first three centuries of Ottoman rule isolated Palestine from most outside influences. The prosperity of 16th-century Ottoman Palestine was followed by an economic and political decline in the 17th century. Ottoman control in the 18th century was indirect. Ḍāhir al-'Umar (c. 1737–75) dominated the political life of northern Palestine for nearly 40 years. Aḥmad al-Jazzār, the Ottoman governor of Acre, had control of most of Palestine, and in 1799, with English and Ottoman help, he successfully defended Acre against Napoleon I.

Both Ḍāhir and al-Jazzār presided over a tightly controlled Palestine, where trade with Europe as well as taxation were growing. They used their new wealth from these sources to gain influence in Istanbul, which allowed them to gain local autonomy and even intermittent control of many areas outside Palestine.

This period came to an end with Napoleon's abortive attempt (1798–1801) to carve for himself a Middle Eastern empire. Egypt, always a determining factor in the fortunes of Palestine, was placed, after the French withdrawal, under the rule of the viceroy Muḥammad (Mehmet) ʿAlī, who soon embarked on a program of expansion at the expense of his Ottoman overlord. In 1831 his armies occupied Palestine, and for nine years he and his son Ibrāhīm gave it a centralizing and modernizing administration.

Their rule increasingly opened the country to Western influences and enabled Christian missionaries to establish many schools; at the same time, however, taxes were increased, and urban rebellions broke out against the harshness of the regime. When in 1840 the British, the Austrians, and the Russians came to the aid of the Ottomans, the Egyptians were forced to withdraw, and Palestine reverted to the Ottoman Empire. Increased European interest, however, led the powers to establish consulates in Jerusalem and in Palestine's port cities.

After 1840 the reforms the sultan promulgated gradually took effect in Palestine. Increased security in the countryside and the Ottoman Land Law of 1858 encouraged the development of private property, agricultural production for the world market, the decline of tribal social organization, growth of the population, and the enrichment of the notable families.

As the Ottomans extended the central government's new military, municipal, judicial, and educational systems to Palestine, the country also witnessed a marked increase in foreign settlements and colonies French, Russian, and German. By far the most important, in spite of their initial numerical insignificance, were the Jewish agricultural settlements, which foreshadowed later Zionist endeavours to establish a Jewish national home and still later a Jewish state (Israel) in Palestine.

The earliest of these settlements was founded by Russian Jews in 1882. In 1896 Theodor Herzl issued a pamphlet entitled Der Judenstaat (The Jewish State) and advocated an autonomous Jewish state, preferably in Palestine. Two years later he himself went to

Palestine to investigate its possibilities and, possibly, to seek the help of the German emperor William II, who was then making a spectacular pilgrimage to the Holy Land.

From 1900 to 1948

In the last years of the 19th century and the early years of the 20th, the Palestinian Arabs shared in a general Arab renaissance. Palestinians found opportunities in the service of the Ottoman Empire, and Palestinian deputies sat in the Ottoman parliaments of 1877, 1908, 1912, and 1914. Several Arabic newspapers appeared in the country before 1914. Their pages reveal that Arab nationalism and opposition to Zionism were strong among some sections of the intelligentsia even before World War I. The Arabs sought an end to Jewish immigration and to land purchases by Zionists.

The number of Zionist colonies, however, mostly subsidized by the French philanthropist Edmond, baron de Rothschild, rose from 19 in 1900 to 47 in 1918, even though the majority of the Jews were town dwellers. The population of Palestine, predominantly agricultural, was about 690,000 in 1914 (535,000 Muslims; 70,000 Christians, most of whom were Arabs; and 85,000 Jews).

World War I and after

During World War I the great powers made a number of decisions concerning the future of Palestine without much regard to the wishes of the indigenous inhabitants. Palestinian Arabs, however, believed that Great Britain had promised them independence in the Ḥusayn-McMahon correspondence, an exchange of letters from July 1915 to March 1916 between Sir Henry McMahon, British high commissioner in Egypt, and Ḥusayn ibn ʿAlī, then emir of Mecca, in which the

British made certain commitments to the Arabs in return for their support against the Ottomans during the war.

Yet by May 1916 Great Britain, France, and Russia had reached an agreement (the Sykes-Picot Agreement) according to which, inter alia, the bulk of Palestine was to be internationalized. Further complicating the situation, in November 1917 Arthur Balfour, the British secretary of state for foreign affairs, addressed a letter to Lord Lionel Walter Rothschild (the Balfour Declaration) expressing sympathy for the establishment in Palestine of a national home for the Jewish people on the understanding that "nothing shall be done which may prejudice the civil and religious rights of existing non-Jewish communities in Palestine."

This declaration did not come about through an act of generosity or stirrings of conscience over the bitter fate of the Jewish people. It was meant, in part, to prompt American Jews to exercise their influence in moving the United States to support British postwar policies as well as to encourage Russian Jews to keep their nation fighting.

Palestine was hard-hit by the war. In addition to the destruction caused by the fighting, the population was devastated by famine, epidemics, and Ottoman punitive measures against Arab nationalists. Major battles took place at Gaza before Jerusalem was captured by British and Allied forces under the command of General Sir Edmund (later 1st Viscount) Allenby in December 1917. The remaining area was occupied by the British by October 1918.

At the war's end, the future of Palestine was problematic. Great Britain, which had set up a military administration in Palestine after capturing Jerusalem, was faced with the problem of having to secure international sanction for the continued occupation of the country in a manner consistent with its ambiguous, seemingly conflicting wartime commitments.

On March 20, 1920, delegates from Palestine attended a general Syrian congress at Damascus, which passed a resolution rejecting the Balfour Declaration and elected Fayṣal I son of Ḥusayn ibn ʿAlī, who ruled the Hejaz king of a united Syria (including Palestine). This resolution echoed one passed earlier in Jerusalem, in February 1919, by the first Palestinian Arab conference of Muslim-Christian associations, which had been founded by leading Palestinian Arab notables to oppose Zionist activities. In April 1920, however, at a peace conference held in San Remo, Italy, the Allies divided the former territories of the defeated Ottoman Empire.

Of the Ottoman provinces in the Syrian region, the northern portion (Syria and Lebanon) was mandated to

France, and the southern portion (Palestine) was mandated to Great Britain. By July 1920 the French had forced Fayṣal to give up his newly founded kingdom of Syria. The hope of founding an Arab Palestine within a federated Syrian state collapsed and with it any prospect of independence. Palestinian Arabs spoke of 1920 as ʿām al-nakbah, the "year of catastrophe."

Uncertainty over the disposition of Palestine affected all its inhabitants and increased political tensions. In April 1920 anti-Zionist riots broke out in the Jewish quarter of Old Jerusalem, killing several and injuring scores. British authorities attributed the riots to Arab disappointment at not having the promises of independence fulfilled and to fears, played on by some Muslim and Christian leaders, of a massive influx of Jews.

Following the confirmation of the mandate at San Remo, the British replaced the military administration with a civilian administration in July 1920, and Sir Herbert (later Viscount) Samuel, a Zionist, was appointed the first high commissioner. The new administration proceeded to implement the Balfour Declaration, announcing in August a quota of 16,500 Jewish immigrants for the first year.

In December 1920, Palestinian Arabs at a congress in Haifa established an executive committee (known as the Arab Executive) to act as the representative of the Arabs. It was never formally recognized by the British and was dissolved in 1934. However, the platform of the Haifa congress, which set out the position that Palestine was an autonomous Arab entity and totally rejected any rights of the Jews to Palestine, remained the basic policy of the Palestinian Arabs until 1948.

The arrival of more than 18,000 Jewish immigrants between 1919 and 1921 and land purchases in 1921 by the Jewish National Fund (established in 1901), which led to the eviction of Arab peasants (fellahin), further aroused Arab opposition that was expressed throughout the region through the Christian-Muslim associations.

On May 1, 1921, more serious anti-Zionist riots broke out in Jaffa, spreading to Petaḥ Tiqwa and other Jewish communities, in which nearly 100 were killed. An Arab delegation of notables visited London in August–November 1921, demanding that the Balfour Declaration be repudiated and proposing the creation of a national government with a parliament democratically elected by the country's Muslims, Christians, and Jews.

Alarmed by the extent of Arab opposition, the British government issued a White Paper in June 1922 declaring that Great Britain did "not contemplate that Palestine as a whole should be converted into a Jewish National Home, but that such a Home should be founded in Palestine." Immigration would not exceed the economic absorptive capacity of the country, and steps would be taken to set up a legislative council.

These proposals were rejected by the Arabs, both because they constituted a large majority of the total mandate population and therefore wished to dominate the instruments of government and rapidly gain independence and because, they argued, the proposals allowed Jewish immigration, which had a political objective, to be regulated by an economic criterion.

The British mandate

In July 1922 the Council of the League of Nations approved the mandate instrument for Palestine, including its preamble incorporating the Balfour Declaration and stressing the Jewish historical connection with Palestine. Article 2 made the mandatory power responsible for placing the country under such "political, administrative and economic conditions as will secure the establishment of the Jewish National Home...and the development of self-governing institutions."

Article 4 allowed for the establishment of a Jewish Agency to advise and cooperate with the Palestine administration in matters affecting the Jewish national home. Article 6 required that the Palestine administration, "while ensuring that the rights and position of other sections of the population are not prejudiced," under suitable conditions should facilitate Jewish immigration and close settlement of Jews on the land.

Although Transjordan i.e., the lands east of the Jordan River constituted three-fourths of the British mandate of Palestine, it was, despite protests from the Zionists, excluded from the clauses covering the establishment of a Jewish national home. On September 29, 1923, the mandate officially came into force.

Palestine was a distinct political entity for the first time in centuries. This created problems and challenges for Palestinian Arabs and Zionists alike. Both communities realized that by the end of the mandate period the region's future would be determined by size of population and ownership of land. Thus the central issues throughout the mandate period were Jewish immigration and land purchases, with the Jews attempting to increase both and the Arabs seeking to slow down or halt both. Conflict over these issues often escalated into violence, and the British were forced to take action a lesson not lost on either side.

Arab nationalist activities became fragmented as tensions arose between clans, religious groups, and city dwellers and fellahin over the issue of how to respond to British rule and the increasing number of

Zionists. Moreover, traditional rivalry between the two old preeminent and ambitious Jerusalem families, the Ḥusaynīs and the Nashāshībīs, whose members had held numerous government posts in the late Ottoman period, inhibited the development of effective Arab leadership. Several Arab organizations in the 1920s opposed Jewish immigration, including the Palestine Arab Congress, Muslim-Christian associations, and the Arab Executive.

Most Arab groups were led by the strongly anti-British Ḥusaynī family, while the National Defense Party (founded 1934) was under the control of the more accommodating Nashāshībī family. In 1921 the British high commissioner appointed Amīn al-Ḥusaynī to be the (grand) mufti of Jerusalem and made him president of the newly formed Supreme Muslim Council, which controlled the Muslim courts and schools and a considerable portion of the funds raised by religious charitable endowments. Amīn al-Ḥusaynī used this religious position to transform himself into the most powerful political figure among the Arabs.

Initially, the Jews of Palestine thought it best served their interests to cooperate with the British administration. The World Zionist Organization (founded 1897) was regarded as the de facto Jewish Agency stipulated in the mandate, although its president, Chaim Weizmann, remained in London, close to the British government; the Polish-born emigré David Ben-Gurion became the leader of a standing executive in Palestine.

Throughout the 1920s most British local authorities in Palestine, especially the military, sympathized with the Palestinian Arabs, whereas the British government in London tended to side with the Zionists. The Jewish community in Palestine, the Yishuv, established its own assembly (Vaʻad Leumi), trade union and labour movement (Histadrut), schools, courts, taxation system, medical services, and a number of industrial enterprises. It also formed a military organization called the Haganah.

The Jewish Agency came to be controlled by a group called the Labour Zionists, who, for the most part, believed in cooperation with the British and Arabs, but another group, the Revisionist Zionists, founded in 1925 and led by Vladimir Jabotinsky, fully realized that their goal of a Jewish state in all of Palestine (i.e., both sides of the Jordan River) was inconsistent with that of Palestinian Arabs. The Revisionists formed their own military arm, Irgun Zvai Leumi, which did not hesitate to use force against the Arabs.

British rule in Palestine during the mandate was, in general, conscientious, efficient, and responsible. The mandate government developed administrative institutions, municipal services, public works, and transport. It laid water pipelines, expanded ports, extended railway lines, and supplied electricity. It was less assiduous in promoting education, however, particularly in the Arab sector, and it was hampered because it had to respond to outbreaks of violence both between the Arab and Jewish communities and against itself. The aims and aspirations of the three parties in Palestine appeared incompatible, which, as events proved, was indeed the case.

There was little political cooperation between Arabs and Jews in Palestine. In 1923 the British high commissioner tried to win Arab cooperation by offers first of a legislative council that would reflect the Arab majority and then of an Arab agency. Both offers were rejected by the Arabs as falling far short of their national demands. Nor did the Arabs wish to legitimize a situation they rejected in principle. The years 1923–29 were relatively quiet; Arab passivity was partly due to the drop in Jewish immigration in 1926–28. In 1927 the number of Jewish emigrants exceeded that of immigrants, and in 1928 there was a net Jewish immigration of only 10 persons.

Nevertheless, the Jewish national home continued to consolidate itself in terms of urban, agricultural, social, cultural, and industrial development. Large amounts of land were purchased from Arab owners, who often were absentee landlords. In August 1929 negotiations were concluded for the formation of an enlarged Jewish Agency to include non-Zionist Jewish sympathizers throughout the world.

This last development, while accentuating Arab fears, gave the Zionists a new sense of confidence. In the same month, a dispute in Jerusalem concerning religious practices at the Western Wall sacred to Jews as the only remnant of the Second Temple of Jerusalem and to Muslims as the site of the Dome of the Rock flared up into serious communal clashes in Jerusalem, Ẕefat, and Hebron. Some 250 were killed and 570 wounded, the Arab casualties being mostly at the hands of British security forces.

A royal commission of inquiry under the aegis of Sir Walter Shaw attributed the clashes to the fact that "the Arabs have come to see in Jewish immigration not only a menace to their livelihood but a possible overlord of the future." A second royal commission, headed by Sir John Hope Simpson, issued a report stating that there was at that time no margin of land available for agricultural settlement by new immigrants.

These two reports raised in an acute form the question of where Britain's duty lay if its specific obligations to the Zionists under the Balfour Declaration clashed with its general obligations to the Arabs under Article 22 of the Covenant of the League of Nations. They also formed the basis of the Passfield White Paper, issued in October 1930, which accorded some priority to Britain's obligations to the Arabs.

Not only did it call for a halt to Jewish immigration, but it also recommended that land be sold only to landless Arabs and that the determination of "economic absorptive capacity" be based on levels of Arab as well as Jewish unemployment. This was seen by the Zionists as cutting at the root of their program, for, if the right of the Arab resident were to gain priority over that of the Jewish immigrant, whether actual or potential, development of the Jewish national home would come to a standstill.

In response to protests from Palestinian Jews and London Zionists, the British prime minister, Ramsay MacDonald, in February 1931 addressed an explanatory letter to Chaim Weizmann nullifying the Passfield White Paper, which virtually meant a return to the policy of the 1922 White Paper. This letter convinced the Arabs that recommendations in their favour made in Palestine could be annulled by Zionist influence at the centre of power in London. In December 1931 a Muslim congress at Jerusalem was attended by delegates from 22 countries to warn against the danger of Zionism.

From the early 1930s onward, developments in Europe once again began to impose themselves more forcefully on Palestine. The Nazi accession to power in Germany in 1933 and the widespread persecution of Jews throughout central and eastern Europe gave a great impetus to Jewish immigration, which jumped to 30,000 in 1933, 42,000 in 1934, and 61,000 in 1935.

By 1936 the Jewish population of Palestine had reached almost 400,000, or one-third of the total. This new wave of immigration provoked major acts of violence against Jews and the British in 1933 and 1935. The Arab population of Palestine also grew rapidly, largely by natural increase, although some Arabs were attracted from outside the region by the capital infusion brought by middle-class Jewish immigrants and British public works.

Most of the Arabs (nearly nine-tenths) continued to be employed in agriculture despite deteriorating economic conditions. By the mid-1930s, however, many landless Arabs had joined the expanding Arab proletariat working in the construction trades on the edge of rapidly growing urban centres. This was the beginning of a shift in the foundations of Palestinian economic and social life that was to have profound immediate and long-term effects.

In November 1935 the Arab political parties collectively demanded that Jewish immigration cease, land transfer be prohibited, and democratic institutions be established. A boycott of Zionist and British goods was proclaimed. In December the British administration offered to set up a legislative council of 28 members, in which the Arabs (both Muslim and Christian) would have a majority. The British would retain control through their selection of nonelected members.

Although Arabs would not be represented in the council in proportion to their numbers, Arab leaders favoured the proposal, but the Zionists criticized it bitterly as an attempt to freeze the national home through a constitutional Arab stranglehold. In any event, London rejected the proposal. This, together with the example of rising nationalism in neighbouring Egypt and Syria, increasing unemployment in Palestine, and a poor citrus harvest, touched off a long-smoldering Arab rebellion.

The Arab Revolt

The Arab Revolt of 1936–39 was the first sustained violent uprising of Palestinian Arabs in more than a century. Thousands of Arabs from all classes were mobilized, and nationalistic sentiment was fanned in the Arabic press, schools, and literary circles. The British, taken aback by the extent and intensity of the revolt, shipped more than 20,000 troops into Palestine, and by 1939 the Zionists had armed more than 15,000 Jews in their own nationalist movement.

The revolt began with spontaneous acts of violence committed by the religiously and nationalistically motivated followers of Sheikh 'Izz al-Dīn al-Qassām, who had been killed by the British in 1935. In April 1936 the murder of two Jews led to escalating violence, and Qassāmite groups initiated a general strike in Jaffa and Nāblus.

At that point the Arab political parties formed an Arab Higher Committee presided over by the mufti of Jerusalem, Amīn al-Ḥusaynī. It called for a general strike, nonpayment of taxes, and the closing of municipal governments (although government employees were allowed to stay at work) and demanded an end to Jewish immigration, a ban on land sales to Jews, and national independence. Simultaneously with the strike, Arab rebels, joined by volunteers from neighbouring Arab countries, took to the hills, attacking Jewish settlements and British installations in the northern part of the country.

By the end of the year, the movement had assumed the dimensions of a national revolt, the mainstay of which was the Arab peasantry. Even though the arrival of British troops restored some semblance of order, the armed rebellion, arson, bombings, and assassinations continued.

A royal commission of inquiry presided over by Lord Robert Peel, which was sent to investigate the volatile situation, reported in July 1937 that the revolt was caused by Arab desire for independence and fear of the Jewish national home. The Peel Commission declared the mandate unworkable and Britain's obligations to Arabs and Jews mutually irreconcilable. In the face of what it described as "right against right," the commission recommended that the region be partitioned. The Zionist attitude toward partition, though ambivalent, was overall one of cautious acceptance. For the first time a British official body explicitly spoke of a Jewish state. The commission not only allotted to this state an area that was immensely larger than the existing Jewish landholdings but recommended the forcible transfer of the Arab population from the proposed Jewish state.

The Zionists, however, still needed mandatory protection for their further development and left the door open for an undivided Palestine. The Arabs were horrified by the idea of dismembering the region and particularly by the suggestion that they be forcibly transferred (to Transjordan). As a result, the momentum of the revolt increased during 1937 and 1938.

In September 1937 the British were forced to declare martial law. The Arab Higher Committee was dissolved, and many officials of the Supreme Muslim Council and other organizations were arrested. The mufti fled to Lebanon and then Iraq, never to return to an undivided Palestine. Although the Arab Revolt continued well into 1939, high casualty rates and firm British measures gradually eroded its strength. According to some estimates, more than 5,000 Arabs were killed, 15,000 wounded, and 5,600 imprisoned during the revolt. Although it signified the birth of a national identity, the revolt was unsuccessful in many ways.

The general strike, which was called off in October 1939, had encouraged Zionist self-reliance, and the Arabs of Palestine were unable to recover from their sustained effort of defying the British administration.

Their traditional leaders were either killed, arrested, or deported, leaving the dispirited and disarmed population divided along urban-rural, class, clan, and religious lines. The Zionists, on the other hand, were united behind Ben-Gurion, and the Haganah had been given permission to arm itself. It cooperated with British forces and the Irgun Zvai Leumi in attacks against Arabs.

However, the prospect of war in Europe alarmed the British government and caused it to reassess its policy in Palestine. If Britain went to war, it could not afford to face Arab hostility in Palestine and in neighbouring countries. The Woodhead Commission, under Sir John Woodhead, was set up to examine the practicality of partition.

In November 1938 it recommended against the Peel Commission's plan largely on the ground that the number of Arabs in the proposed Jewish state would be almost equal to the number of Jews and put forward alternative proposals drastically reducing the area of the Jewish state and limiting the sovereignty of the proposed states. This was unacceptable to both Arabs and Jews. Seeking to find a solution acceptable to both parties, the British announced the impracticability of partition and called for a roundtable conference in London.

No agreement was reached at the London conference held during February and March 1939. In May 1939, however, the British government issued a White Paper, which essentially yielded to Arab demands. It stated that the Jewish national home should be established within an independent Palestinian state.

During the next five years 75,000 Jews would be allowed into the country; thereafter Jewish immigration would be subject to Arab "acquiescence." Land transfer to Jews would be allowed only in certain areas in Palestine, and an independent Palestinian state would be considered within 10 years. The Arabs, although in favour of the new policy, rejected the White Paper, largely because they mistrusted the British government and opposed a provision contained in the paper for extending the mandate beyond the 10-year period.

The Zionists were shocked and enraged by the paper, which they considered a death blow to their program and to Jews who desperately sought refuge in Palestine from the growing persecution they were enduring in Europe. The 1939 White Paper marked the end of the Anglo-Zionist entente.

Progress toward a Jewish national home had, however, been remarkable since 1918. Although the majority of the Jewish population was urban, the number of rural Zionist colonies had increased from 47 to about 200. Between 1922 and 1940 Jewish landholdings had risen from about 148,500 to 383,500 acres (about 60,100 to 155,200 hectares) and now constituted roughly one-seventh of the cultivatable land, and the Jewish population had grown from 83,790 to some 467,000, or nearly one-third of a total population of about 1,528,000.

Tel Aviv had developed into an all-Jewish city of 150,000 inhabitants, and hundreds of millions of dollars of Jewish capital had been introduced into the region. The Jewish literacy rate was high, schools were expanding, and the Hebrew language had become widespread. Despite a split in 1935 between the mainline Zionists and the radical Revisionists, who advocated the use of force to establish the Zionist state, Zionist institutions in Palestine became stronger in the 1930s and helped create the preconditions for the establishment of a Jewish state.

World War II

With the outbreak of World War II in September 1939, Zionist and British policies came into direct conflict. Throughout the war Zionists sought with growing urgency to increase Jewish immigration to Palestine, while the British sought to prevent such immigration, regarding it as illegal and a threat to the stability of a region essential to the war effort. Ben-Gurion declared on behalf of the Jewish Agency:

"We shall fight [beside Great Britain in] this war as if there was no White Paper and we shall fight the White Paper as if there was no war." British attempts to prevent Jewish immigration to Palestine in the face of the Holocaust the terrible tragedy befalling European Jewry and others deemed undesirable by the Nazis led to the disastrous sinking of two ships carrying Jewish refugees, the Patria (November 1940) and the Struma (February 1942).

In response, the Irgun, under the leadership of Menachem Begin, and a small terrorist splinter group, LEHI (Fighters for the Freedom of Israel), known for its founder as the Stern Gang, embarked on widespread attacks on the British, culminating in the murder of Lord Moyne, British minister of state, by two LEHI members in Cairo in November 1944.

During the war years the Jewish community in Palestine was vastly strengthened. Its moderate wing supported the British; in September 1944 a Jewish brigade was formed a total of 27,000 Jews having enlisted in the British forces and attached to the British 8th Army. Jewish industry in general was given immense impetus by the war, and a Jewish munitions industry developed to manufacture antitank mines for the British forces. For the Yishuv the war and the Holocaust confirmed that a Jewish state must be established in Palestine. Important also was the support of American Zionists. In May 1942, at a Zionist conference held at the Biltmore Hotel in New York City, Ben-Gurion gained support for a program demanding unrestricted immigration, a Jewish army, and the establishment of Palestine as a Jewish commonwealth.

The Arabs of Palestine remained largely quiescent throughout the war. Amīn al-Ḥusaynī had fled by way of Iraq, Iran, Turkey, and Italy to Germany, whence he broadcast appeals to his fellow Arabs to ally with the Axis powers against Britain and Zionism. Yet the mufti failed to rally Palestinian Arabs to the Axis cause. Although some supported Germany, the majority supported the Allies, and approximately 23,000 Arabs enlisted in the British forces (especially in the Arab Legion).

Increases in agricultural prices benefited the Arab peasants, who began to pay accumulated debts. However, the Arab Revolt had ruined many Arab merchants and importers, and British war activities, although bringing new levels of prosperity, further weakened the traditional social institutions the family and village by fostering a large urban Arab working class.

The Allied discovery of the Nazi extermination camps at the end of World War II and the undecided future of Holocaust survivors led to an increasing number of pro-Zionist statements from U.S. politicians. In August 1945 U.S. President Harry S. Truman requested that British Prime Minister Clement Attlee facilitate the immediate admission of 100,000 Jewish Holocaust survivors into Palestine, and in December the U.S. Senate and House of Representatives asked for unrestricted Jewish immigration to the limit of the economic absorptive capacity of Palestine. Truman's request signaled the U.S. entry into the arena of powers determining the future of Palestine. The question of Palestine, now linked with the fate of Holocaust survivors, became once again the focus of international attention.

As the war came to an end, the neighbouring Arab countries began to take a more direct interest in Palestine. In October 1944 Arab heads of state met in Alexandria, Egypt, and issued a statement, the Alexandria Protocol, setting out the Arab position. They made clear that, although they regretted the bitter fate inflicted upon European Jewry by European dictatorships, the issue of European Jewish survivors ought not to be confused with Zionism.

Solving the problem of European Jewry, they asserted, should not be achieved by inflicting injustice on Palestinian Arabs. The covenant of the League of Arab States, or Arab League, formed in March 1945, contained an annex emphasizing the Arab character of Palestine. The Arab League appointed an Arab Higher Executive for Palestine (the Arab Higher Committee), which included a broad spectrum of Palestinian leaders, to speak for the Palestinian Arabs. In December 1945 the league declared a boycott of

Zionist goods. The pattern of the postwar struggle for Palestine was unmistakably emerging.

The early postwar period

The major issue between 1945 and 1948 was, as it had been throughout the mandate, Jewish immigration to Palestine. The Yishuv was determined to remove all restrictions to Jewish immigration and to establish a Jewish state. The Arabs were determined that no more Jews should arrive and that Palestine should achieve independence as an Arab state. The primary goal of British policy following World War II was to secure British strategic interests in the Middle East and Asia. Because the cooperation of the Arab states was considered essential to this goal, British Foreign Secretary Ernest Bevin opposed Jewish immigration and the foundation of an independent Jewish state in Palestine. The U.S. State Department basically supported the British position, but Truman was determined to ensure that Jews displaced by the war were permitted to enter Palestine. The issue was resolved in 1948 when the British mandate collapsed under the pressure of force and diplomacy.

In November 1945, in an effort to secure American coresponsibility for a Palestinian policy, Bevin announced the formation of an Anglo-American Committee of Inquiry. Pending the report of the committee, Jewish immigration would continue at the rate of 1,500 persons per month above the 75,000 limit set by the 1939 White Paper. A plan of provincial autonomy for Arabs and Jews was worked out in an Anglo-American conference in 1946 and became the basis for discussions in London between Great Britain and the representatives of Arabs and Zionists.

In the meantime, Zionist pressure in Palestine was intensified by the unauthorized immigration of refugees on a hitherto unprecedented scale and by closely coordinated attacks by Zionist underground forces. Jewish immigration was impelled by the burning memories of the Holocaust, the chaotic postwar conditions in Europe, and the growing possibility of attaining a Jewish state where the victims of persecution could guarantee their own safety. The underground's attacks culminated in Jerusalem on July 22, 1946, when the Irgun blew up a part of the King David Hotel containing British government and military offices, with the loss of 91 lives.

On the Arab side, a meeting of the Arab states took place in June 1946 at Blūdān, Syria, at which secret resolutions were adopted threatening British and American interests in the Middle East if Arab rights were disregarded. In Palestine the Ḥusaynīs consolidated their power, despite widespread mistrust of the mufti, who now resided in Egypt.

While Zionists pressed ahead with immigration and attacks on the government, and Arab states mobilized in response, British resolve to remain in the Middle East was collapsing. World War II had left Britain victorious but exhausted. After the war it lacked the funds and political will to maintain control of colonial possessions that were agitating, with increasing violence, for independence. When a conference called in London in February 1947 failed to resolve the impasse, Great Britain, already negotiating its withdrawal from India and eager to decrease its costly military presence in Palestine (of the more than 280,000 troops stationed there during the war, more than 80,000 still remained), referred the Palestine question to the United Nations (UN).

On August 31, 1947, a majority report of the UN Special Committee on Palestine (UNSCOP) recommended that the region be partitioned into an Arab and a Jewish state, which, however, should retain an economic union. Jerusalem and its environs were to be international. These recommendations were substantially adopted by a two-thirds majority of the UN General Assembly in Resolution 181, dated November 29, 1947, a decision made possible partly because of an agreement between the United States and the Soviet Union on partition and partly because pressure was exerted on some small countries by Zionist sympathizers in the United States. All the Islamic Asian countries voted against partition, and an Arab proposal to query the International Court of Justice on the competence of the General Assembly to partition a country against the wishes of the majority of its inhabitants (in 1946 there were 1,269,000 Arabs and 678,000 Jews in Palestine) was narrowly defeated.

The Zionists welcomed the partition proposal both because it recognized a Jewish state and because it allotted slightly more than half of (west-of-Jordan) Palestine to it. As in 1937, the Arabs fiercely opposed partition both in principle and because nearly half of the population of the Jewish state would be Arab. Resolution 181 called for the formation of the UN Palestine Commission which it tasked with selecting and overseeing provisional councils of government for the Jewish and Arab states by April 1, 1948 and set the date for the termination of the mandate no later than August 1, 1948. (The British later announced that the mandate would be terminated on May 15, 1948.)

Civil war in Palestine

Soon after the UN resolution, fighting broke out in Palestine. The Zionists mobilized their forces and redoubled their efforts to bring in immigrants. In December 1947 the Arab League pledged its support to the Palestinian Arabs and organized a force of 3,000 volunteers. Civil war spread, and external intervention increased as the disintegration of the British administration progressed.

Alarmed by the continued fighting, the United States in early March 1948 expressed its opposition to forcibly implementing a partition. A March 12 report by the UN Palestine Commission stated that the establishment of provisional councils of government able to fulfill their functions would be impossible by April 1. Arab resistance to the partition in principle precluded the establishment of an Arab council, and, although steps had been taken toward the selection of the Jewish council, the commission reported that the latter council would be unable to carry out its functions as intended by the resolution.

Hampering efforts altogether was Great Britain's refusal in any case to share with the commission the administration of Palestine during the transitional period. On March 19 the United States called for the UN Palestine Commission to suspend its efforts. On March 30 the United States proposed that a truce be declared and that the problem be further considered by the General Assembly.

The Zionists, insisting that partition was binding and anxious about the change in U.S. policy, made a major effort to establish their state. They launched two offensives during April. The success of these operations coincided roughly with the failure of an Arab attack on the Zionist settlement of Mishmar Ha ʿEmeq; the death in battle of an Arab national hero, ʿAbd al-Qādir al-Ḥusaynī, in command of the Jerusalem front; and the massacre, by Irgunists and members of the Stern Gang, of civilian inhabitants of the Arab village of Dayr Yāsīn. On April 22 Haifa fell to the Zionists, and Jaffa, after severe mortar shelling, surrendered to them on May 13. Simultaneously with their military offensives, the Zionists launched a campaign of psychological warfare. The Arabs of Palestine, divided, badly led, and reliant on the regular armies of the Arab states, became demoralized, and their efforts to prevent partition collapsed.

On May 14 the last British high commissioner, General Sir Alan Cunningham, left Palestine. On the same day the State of Israel was declared and within a few hours won de facto recognition from the United States and de jure recognition from the Soviet Union. Early on May 15 units of the regular armies of Syria, Transjordan, Iraq, and Egypt crossed the frontiers of Palestine.

In a series of campaigns alternating with truces between May and December 1948, the Arab units were routed, and by the summer of 1949 Israel had concluded armistices with its neighbours. It had also been recognized by more than 50 governments throughout the world, joined the United Nations, and established its sovereignty over about 8,000 square miles (21,000 square km) of formerly mandated

Palestine west of the Jordan River. The remaining 2,000 square miles (5,200 square km) were divided between Transjordan and Egypt.

Transjordan retained the lands on the west bank of the Jordan River, including the eastern portion of Jerusalem (East Jerusalem), although its annexation of those lands in 1950 was not generally recognized as legitimate. In 1949 the name of the expanded country was changed to the Hashimite Kingdom of Jordan. Egypt retained control of, but did not annex, a small area on the Mediterranean coast that became known as the Gaza Strip. The Palestinian Arab community ceased to exist as a cohesive social and political entity.

Palestine and the Palestinians (1948–67)

The partition of Palestine and its aftermath

If one chief theme in the post-1948 pattern was embattled Israel and a second the hostility of its Arab neighbours, a third was the plight of the huge number of Arab refugees. The violent birth of Israel led to a major displacement of the Arab population, who either were driven out by Zionist military forces before May 15, 1948, or by the Israeli army after that date or fled for fear of violence by these forces.

Many wealthy merchants and leading urban notables from Jaffa, Tel Aviv, Haifa, and Jerusalem fled to Lebanon, Egypt, and Jordan, while the middle class tended to move to all-Arab towns such as Nāblus and Nazareth. The majority of fellahin ended up in refugee camps. More than 400 Arab villages disappeared, and Arab life in the coastal cities (especially Jaffa and Haifa) virtually disintegrated. The centre of Palestinian life shifted to the Arab towns of the hilly eastern portion of the region which was immediately west of the Jordan River and came to be called the West Bank.

Like everything else in the Arab-Israeli conflict, population figures are hotly disputed. Nearly 1,400,000 Arabs lived in Palestine when the war broke out. Estimates of the number of Arabs displaced from their original homes, villages, and neighbourhoods during the period from December 1947 to January 1949 range from about 520,000 to about 1,000,000; there is general consensus, however, that the actual number was more than 600,000 and likely exceeded 700,000. Some 276,000 moved to the West Bank; by 1949 more than half the prewar Arab population of Palestine lived in the West Bank (from 400,000 in 1947 to more than 700,000). Between 160,000 and 190,000 fled to the Gaza Strip. More than one-fifth of Palestinian Arabs left Palestine altogether. About 100,000 of these went to Lebanon, 100,000 to Jordan, between 75,000 and 90,000 to Syria, 7,000 to 10,000 to Egypt, and 4,000 to Iraq.

The term "Palestinian"

Henceforth the term Palestinian will be used when referring to the Arabs of the former mandated Palestine, excluding Israel. Although the Arabs of Palestine had been creating and developing a Palestinian identity for about 200 years, the idea that Palestinians form a distinct people is relatively recent. The Arabs living in Palestine had never had a separate state.

Until the establishment of Israel, the term Palestinian was used by Jews and foreigners to describe the inhabitants of Palestine and had only begun to be used by the Arabs themselves at the turn of the 20th century; at the same time, most saw themselves as part of the larger Arab or Muslim community.

The Arabs of Palestine began widely using the term Palestinian starting in the pre-World War I period to indicate the nationalist concept of a Palestinian people.

But after 1948 and even more so after 1967 for Palestinians themselves the term came to signify not only a place of origin but, more importantly, a sense of a shared past and future in the form of a Palestinian state.

Diverging histories for Palestinian Arabs

The Israeli Arabs

Approximately 150,000 Arabs remained in Israel when the Israeli state was founded. These Israeli Arabs represented about one-eighth of all Palestinians and by 1952 roughly the same proportion of the Israeli population. The majority of them lived in villages in western Galilee. Because much of their land was confiscated, Arabs were forced to abandon agriculture and become unskilled wage laborers, working in Jewish industries and construction companies.

As citizens of the State of Israel, in theory they were guaranteed equal religious and civil rights with Jews. In reality, however, until 1966 they lived under a military jurisdiction that imposed severe restrictions on their political options and freedom of movement. Most of them remained politically quiescent, and many accepted Zionist Israel as a reality and sought to ameliorate their circumstances through electoral participation, education, and economic integration.

Israel sought to impede the development of a cohesive national consciousness among the Palestinians by dealing with various minority groups, such as Druze, Circassians, and Bedouin; by hindering the work of the Muslim religious organizations; by arresting and harassing individuals suspected of harbouring nationalist sentiments; and by focusing on education as a means of creating a new Israeli Arab identity. By the late 1960s, as agriculture declined and social customs related to such events as bride selection and marriage broke down, the old patriarchal clan system had all but collapsed. For almost 20 years after Israel was established, Israeli Arabs were isolated from other Arabs.

West Bank (and Jordanian) Palestinians

The Jordanian monarchy saw in the events of 1948–49 the opportunity to expand Jordanian territory and to integrate Palestinians into its population and thereby create a new Jordanian nationality. Through a series of political and social policies, Jordan sought to consolidate its control over the political future of Palestinians and to become their speaker. It provided education and, in 1949, extended citizenship to Palestinians; indeed, a majority of all Palestinians became Jordanian citizens.

However, tensions soon developed between original Jordanian citizens and the better-educated, more skilled newcomers. Wealthy Palestinians lived in the towns of the eastern and western sides of the Jordan River, competing for positions within the government, while the fellahin filled the UN refugee camps.

Palestinians constituted about two-thirds of the population of Jordan. Half the seats in the Jordanian Chamber of Deputies were reserved for representatives from the West Bank, but this measure and similar attempts to integrate the West Bank with the area lying east of the Jordan River were made difficult by the significant social, economic, educational, and political differences between the residents of each. Jordanian Palestinians, other than the notable families favoured by the Jordanian monarchy, tended to support the radical pan-Arab and anti-Israeli policies of Egypt's President Gamal Abdel Nasser rather than the more cautious and conciliatory position of Jordan's King Ḥussein.

Palestinians in the Gaza Strip

During the 20 years the Gaza Strip was under Egyptian control (1948–67), it remained little more than a reservation. Egyptian rule was generally repressive. Palestinians living in the region were denied citizenship, which rendered them stateless (i.e., it left them without citizenship of any nation), and they were allowed little real control over local administration. They were, however, allowed to attend Egyptian universities and, at times, to elect local officials.

In 1948 Amīn al-Ḥusaynī declared a Government of All Palestine in the Gaza Strip. However, because it was totally dependent on Egypt, it was short-lived. The failure of this venture and al-Ḥusaynī's lack of credibility because of his collaboration with the Axis powers during World War II did much to weaken Palestinian Arab nationalism in the 1950s.

The Gaza Strip, 25 miles (40 km) long and 4–5 miles (6–8 km) wide, became one of the most densely populated areas of the world, with more than four-fifths of its population urban. Poverty and social misery became characteristic of life in the region. The rate of unemployment was high; many of the Palestinians lived in refugee camps, depending primarily on UN aid (see below). Most of the agricultural lands they had formerly worked were now inaccessible, and little or no industry was allowed, but commerce flourished as Gaza became a kind of duty-free port for Egyptians. Although some Gaza Strip Palestinians were able to leave the territory and gain an education and find employment elsewhere, most had no alternative but to stay in the area, despite its lack of natural resources and jobs.

The UNRWA camps

In December 1949 the UN General Assembly created the United Nations Relief and Works Agency for Palestine Refugees in the Near East (UNRWA) to assist the Palestinian refugees. In May 1950 UNRWA established a total of 53 refugees "camps" on both sides of the Jordan River and in the Gaza Strip, Lebanon, and Syria to assist the 650,000 or more Arab refugees it calculated needed help. Initially refugees in the improvised camps lived in tents, but after 1958 these were replaced by small houses of concrete blocks with iron roofs.

Conditions were extremely harsh; often several families had to share one tent, and exposure to the extreme winter and summer temperatures inflicted additional suffering. Loss of home and income lowered morale. Although the refugees were provided with rent-free accommodations and basic services such as water, health care, and education (UNRWA ran both elementary and secondary schools in the camps, teaching more than 40,000 students by 1951), poverty and misery were widespread. Work was scarce, even though UNRWA sought to integrate the Palestinians into the depressed economies of the "host" countries.

Palestinians who continued to live in refugee camps felt a greater sense of alienation and dislocation than the more fortunate ones who found jobs and housing and became integrated into the national economies of the countries in which they resided. Although the camps strengthened family and village ties, their demoralized inhabitants were isolated from mainstream Palestinian political activities during the 1950s.

Palestinians outside mandated Palestine

Palestinians found employment in Syria, Iraq, Lebanon, and the Persian Gulf states, but only a few were able to become citizens of those countries. Often they were the victims of discrimination, as well as being closely supervised by the respective governments intent on limiting their political activities.

Resurgence of Palestinian identity

The events of 1948 (also called by Palestinians al-nakbah, "the catastrophe") and the experience of exile shaped Palestinian political and cultural activity for the next generation. The central task of reconstruction fell to Palestinians living outside Israel both in the West Bank and Gaza communities and in the new Palestinian communities outside the former British mandate. (Arabs living within the State of Israel remained in an ambiguous, isolated situation and were regarded with some suspicion by both Israelis and Palestinians.)

The new leaders came disproportionately from among those who had moved to various Middle Eastern states and to the West, even though four out of five

Palestinians had remained within the borders of the former British mandate. By the mid-1960s, despite Israeli efforts to forestall the emergence of a new Palestinian identity, a young, educated leadership had arisen, replacing the discredited traditional local and clan leaders.

The role of camps

Palestinian refugee camps differed depending on the country in which they were located, but they shared one common development the emergence of a "diaspora consciousness." In time this consciousness grew into a renewed national identity and reinvigorated social institutions, leading to the establishment of more complex social and political structures by the 1960s.

A new Palestinian leadership emerged from the schools UNRWA had established, as well as from the universities of Egypt, Syria, Lebanon, western Europe, and the United States. Palestinians living in the UNRWA-administered refugee camps felt isolated, politically powerless, disoriented, bitter, and resentful. They remained unassimilated and were generating a new sense of identity based on a pan-Arabism inspired by Nasser, the cultivated memory of a lost paradise (Palestine), and an emerging pan-Islamic movement.

The role of Palestinians outside formerly mandated Palestine

By the late 1960s a class of educated and mobile Palestinians had emerged, with fewer than half of them living in the West Bank or Gaza. They were working in the oil companies, civil services, and educational institutions of most Arab states in the Middle East. Having successfully resisted the efforts of Amīn al-Ḥusaynī, Jordan, and Egypt to control and speak for them, they joined the process of reshaping

Palestinian consciousness and institutions. Thus Palestinians entered a new stage of the struggle for nationhood.

The Palestine Liberation Organization

An Arab summit meeting in Cairo in 1964 led to the formation of the Palestine Liberation Organization (PLO). A political umbrella organization of several Palestinian groups, the PLO thereafter consistently claimed to be the sole representative of all Palestinian people. Its first leader was Aḥmad Shuqayrī, a protégé of Egypt. In its charter (the Palestine National Charter, or Covenant) the PLO delineated its basic principles and goals, the most important of which were the right to an independent state, the total liberation of Palestine, and the destruction of the State of Israel.

A Palestine National Council (PNC) was established to serve as the supreme body, or parliament, of the PLO, and an executive committee was formed to manage PLO activities. Initially, the PNC consisted of civilian representatives from various areas, including Jordan, the West Bank, and the Persian Gulf states, but representatives of guerrilla organizations were added in 1968.

Fatah and other guerrilla organizations

Several years before the creation of the PLO, a secret organization had been formed: the Palestine National Liberation Movement (Ḥarakat al-Taḥrīr al-Waṭanī al-Filasṭīnī), known from a reversal of its Arabic initials as Fatah. Both the PLO and Fatah undertook the training of guerrilla units for raids on Israel. In addition to Fatah, the largest and most influential guerrilla organization, several others emerged in the late 1960s.

The most important ones were the Popular Front for the Liberation of Palestine (PFLP), the Democratic

Front for the Liberation of Palestine (DFLP), the Popular Front for the Liberation of Palestine–General Command (PFLP–GC, a splinter group from the PFLP), and al-Ṣāʿiqah (backed by Syria). These groups joined forces inside the PLO despite their differences in ideology and tactics (some were dedicated to openly terrorist tactics). In 1969 Yasser Arafat, leader of Fatah, became chairman of the PLO's executive committee and thus the chief of the Palestinian national movement.

Despite their differences in tactics and ideology, the guerrilla organizations were united in rejecting any political settlement that did not include what they characterized as the total liberation of Palestine and the return of the refugees to their homeland, goals that were to be achieved through armed struggle. Palestinian spokesmen claimed, however, that, while they aimed at dismantling Israel and purging Palestine of Zionism, they also sought to establish a nonsectarian state in which Jews, Christians, and Muslims could live in equality. Most Israelis doubted the sincerity or practicality of this goal and viewed the PLO as a terrorist organization committed to destroying not only the Zionist state but Israeli Jews.

The Arab-Israeli war of 1967 and its consequences

In the Arab-Israeli war of 1967, Israel defeated the combined forces of Egypt, Syria, and Jordan and also overran large tracts of territory, including East Jerusalem, the West Bank (known to Israelis by the biblical names Judaea and Samaria), and Gaza. Israel's victory gave rise to another exodus of Palestinians, with more than 250,000 people fleeing to the eastern bank of the Jordan River. However, roughly 600,000 Palestinians remained in the West Bank and 300,000 in Gaza.

Thus the 3,000,000 Israeli Jews came to rule some 1,200,000 Arabs (including the 300,000 already living in the State of Israel). Moreover, a movement developed among Israelis who advocated settling the occupied territories particularly the West Bank as part of the Jewish patrimony in the Holy Land. Several thousand Israeli Jews settled in the territories in the decade following the war.

Israeli Arabs

In the years following the 1967 war, circumstances changed dramatically for Israeli Arabs. As a result of their resumed contact with the Palestinians of the West Bank and the Gaza Strip, they began to recover from their long period of inactivity. Following the Arab-Israeli war of 1973, Arab Israelis played a greater role in Israeli institutions. They also were significantly affected by Israel's economic prosperity; by the 1980s the Arab economy had gained some autonomy, as

Arabs moved from unskilled work to business ownership.

The PLO's rise as a revolutionary force

Throughout the 1970s and '80s the PLO, dominated by Fatah, acted as a state in the making, launching frequent military attacks on Israel. The strategy of armed struggle had been inaugurated as early as the 1950s, and, indeed, guerrilla raids against military and civilian targets in Israel had been a factor leading to the Suez crisis of 1956 and the 1967 war. However, after 1967 Fatah launched a new wave of violent activities, and the Palestinian guerrilla groups, under the umbrella of the PLO, emerged as an element of major importance in the Middle East.

The Arab-Israeli war had discredited Nasser's Pan-Arabism, and Fatah quickly permeated and mobilized the reunited Palestinian population, providing social services and organizations. One result was an escalating cycle of raids and reprisals between the Palestinian guerrillas and Israel; guerrilla attacks on Israeli occupation forces and terror attacks on Israeli civilians (defended by the PLO until renounced by Arafat in 1988) became a key element in the struggle against Israel.

The PLO's struggle for Palestinian autonomy

Although generally recognized as the symbol of the Palestinian national movement, the PLO lacked organizational cohesion. It championed Palestinian distinctiveness and autonomy, but circumstances forced the leadership to remain somewhat distant from the lives of Palestinians. This made it difficult to impose a unified policy. A major problem for the PLO was gaining autonomy in order to pursue Palestinian interests, especially since the effort to do so inevitably brought the organization into conflict with the Arab states in which Palestinians lived.

Palestinians and the PLO in Jordan

Within Jordan an understanding was reached whereby the royal government allowed the Palestinian guerrillas independent control of their own bases in the Jordan Valley, but relations between the government and the guerrillas remained uneasy. The guerrillas suspected King Ḥussein who had to face the damage inflicted upon his country by Israeli reprisals of preparing to reach a direct settlement with Israel at their expense.

Tensions between the Jordanian army loyal to King Ḥussein and the Palestinian guerrillas erupted in a brief but bloody civil war in September 1970 that became known as "Black September." On September 6–9 the PFLP hijacked to a Jordanian airstrip three airliners (American, Swiss, and British) with a total of more than

300 people aboard. The hijackers threatened to destroy the aircraft, with the passengers aboard, unless Palestinian guerrillas detained in Europe and Israel were released. All the passengers were freed by September 30, when the PFLP secured its main demands (after destroying the airliners). Full warfare ensued when the Jordanian army moved against the guerrillas.

By September 17 the army was fighting the guerrillas in Amman and in northern Jordan, where the guerrillas were reinforced by Syria-based armoured units of the Palestine Liberation Army a body ostensibly part of the PLO but in fact controlled by Syria. Hostilities formally ended on September 25, with the guerrillas still in control of their northern strongholds.

Total casualties were variously estimated at 1,000 to 5,000 people killed and up to 10,000 injured. In 1971, however, the fighting resumed, and the Jordanian army established full control over the whole country and crushed the Palestinian military. From that point on, the king and the PLO were deeply suspicious of each other, and the majority of Palestinians holding Jordanian citizenship, especially those living on the West Bank under Israeli control, became highly critical of the king and his policies.

Palestinians and the PLO in Lebanon

Driven from Jordan, the PLO intensified its activities in Lebanon. The presence of more than 235,000 Palestinians was a source of tension and conflict in Lebanon, as it had been in Jordan. Palestinians had few rights, and most worked for low wages in poor conditions. Palestinian guerrillas continued to carry out attacks against Israel. Israel countered with raids, primarily into southern Lebanon. The Lebanese government sought to restrict the activities of the

Palestinian guerrillas, which led to sporadic fighting between the Lebanese army and the guerrillas.

In 1973 the Palestinian movement suffered a severe blow from an Israeli commando attack in Beirut in April that killed three of its leaders. Following the attack, the Lebanese army assaulted guerrilla bases and refugee camps throughout the country. An agreement was reached requiring the Palestinians to limit their activities to border areas near Israel and refugee camps near urban centres. After 1973 many Palestinians from Lebanon and Jordan moved to the increasingly prosperous and labour-hungry Arab oil states, such as Kuwait and Saudi Arabia.

International recognition

The PLO made important gains in its international relations during the 1970s. By the end of the decade the organization had representatives in more than 80 countries. On September 22, 1974, the UN General Assembly, overriding strong Israeli objections, included on its agenda for the first time the "Palestine question" as a separate subject for debate rather than as part of the general question of the Middle East. On November 13 the assembly heard Arafat plead for the Palestinian people's national rights.

International recognition of the PLO had important repercussions within the Arab camp. At an Arab summit conference held in Rabat, Morocco, on October 26–28, 1974, King Ḥussein accepted a resolution stating that any "liberated" Palestinian territory "should revert to its legitimate Palestinian owners under the leadership of the PLO." The Rabat decision was denounced by the more radical "rejection front," composed of the PFLP, the PFLP–GC, the pro-Iraq Arab Liberation Front, and the Front for the Popular Palestinian Struggle, which sought to regain all of Palestine. Although the decision was recognized as enhancing the less extreme position of the PLO elements led by Arafat, the United States continued adamantly to refuse to recognize or deal with the PLO so long as the PLO refused to recognize Israel's right to exist.

Palestinians and the civil war in Lebanon

Palestinian guerrilla activity against Israel in 1975 was largely confined to the southern Lebanese border area, where it provoked heavy Israeli attacks from air, land, and sea against Palestinian refugee camps that the Israelis alleged were being used as guerrilla bases. Israeli raids, however, were overshadowed by growing civil strife in Lebanon that developed along Muslim-Christian lines. Civil war between the militias of Lebanon's sectarian groups erupted in 1975, bringing 15 years of bloodshed, in which more than 100,000 people were killed. The presence of Palestinians was a factor contributing to the civil war, and the war proved disastrous for them.

The PLO initially tried to stay out of the fighting, but by the end of 1975 groups within the overall organization, particularly the "rejection front" groups, were being drawn into an alliance with the Muslim and leftist groups fighting against the Christians. Fighting broke out throughout the country during the first half of January 1976 as Christian forces, foremost the right-wing Maronite Phalange, blockaded the Palestinian refugee camps, and the Palestinian forces and their Lebanese allies responded by attacking Christian villages on the coast.

Intense fighting continued, and the PLO, despite all efforts, proved unable to protect the Palestinian population. In August, after a two-month siege, Christian forces killed an estimated 2,000 to 3,000 Palestinians in the Tall al-Zaʻtar camp northeast of

Beirut. A peace agreement was negotiated in October 1976. The settlement provided for the creation of a 30,000-member Arab Deterrent Force (ADF), a cease-fire throughout the country, withdrawal of forces to positions held before April 1975, and implementation of a 1969 agreement limiting Palestinian guerrilla operations in Lebanon.

Although the Palestinian guerrillas suffered heavy losses in the Lebanese civil war, they continued to mount attacks against Israel in the late 1970s. Israel again responded with raids into southern Lebanon. In September 1977 Israeli troops crossed into southern Lebanon to support right-wing Christian forces. On March 11, 1978, a Palestinian raid into Israel killed three dozen civilian tourists and wounded some 80 others, and Israel invaded southern Lebanon three days later (Operation Litani).

On March 19 the UN Security Council passed resolution 425, calling for Israel to withdraw and establishing the UN Interim Force in Lebanon (UNIFIL). The Israelis withdrew their forces only partially and continued to occupy a strip of Lebanese territory along the southern frontier, in violation of this resolution. They had been only partly successful in their aim of destroying Palestinian guerrillas and their bases south of the Litani River. Several hundred of the Palestinian guerrillas had been killed, but most of them had escaped northward. Estimates of civilian casualties ranged from 1,000 to 2,000.

The PLO in the occupied territories

Under the Likud Party government of the late 1970s and early '80s, Israel's settlements in the West Bank grew dramatically, as part of a new Likud policy to maintain strategic dominance in the area. The growth in settlements was accompanied by an increase in

Israeli control over the territories, and large parts of those territories were incorporated into Israel's infrastructure. As this occupation solidified, many local Palestinian leaders turned to building social organizations, labour unions, and religious, educational, and political institutions.

The PLO responded by making its presence increasingly felt in the occupied territories, building its own youth groups, providing families with economic assistance, and putting in place a rival political infrastructure that made it possible for PLO-supported candidates to win in the municipal elections of 1976. By the early 1980s the PLO had set up an extensive bureaucratic structure that provided health, housing, educational, legal, media, and labour services for Palestinians both inside and outside the camps. Israeli and Jordanian attempts to encourage alternatives to the PLO failed in the 1980s. Active opposition to Israeli control in the West Bank spread, while frequent demonstrations, strikes, and other incidents occurred, particularly among students.

Negotiations, violence, and incipient self-rule

The late 1970s was a period of more active negotiation on Arab-Israeli disputes. The Arab states supported Palestinian participation in an overall settlement providing for Israeli withdrawal from areas occupied since the 1967 war and establishing a Palestinian state in the West Bank and the Gaza Strip. The U.S. position toward the Palestinians showed signs of softening. In March 1977 U.S. President Jimmy Carter spoke of the need for a Palestinian homeland, and he later stated that it was essential for the Palestinians to take part in the peace process. The Israeli cabinet continued to reject the participation of the PLO in the peace process but agreed not to look too closely at the background of

Palestinians who might become members of delegations from Arab countries.

The Camp David Accords and the PLO

In November 1977 the Egyptian president, Anwar Sadat, initiated peace negotiations that led to the agreement known as the Camp David Accords in September 1978 and to the Egyptian-Israeli peace treaty signed on March 26, 1979. Provisions of the accords (named for Camp David, Maryland, U.S., where they were negotiated) included the establishment of a self-governing authority in the West Bank and the Gaza Strip and a transitional period of not more than five years, at the end of which the inhabitants would become autonomous. The Soviet Union during the time of the peace negotiations recognized the PLO as the sole legitimate representative of the Palestinians and in 1981 extended formal diplomatic recognition. The nations of western Europe announced their support of PLO participation in peace negotiations in June 1980. The PLO continued to seek diplomatic recognition from the United States, but the Carter administration honoured a secret commitment the former U.S. secretary of state Henry Kissinger made to Israel not to deal with the PLO so long as it declined to renounce terrorism and to recognize Israel's right to exist.

The dispersal of the PLO from Lebanon

The Likud Party government of Israel viewed the possibility of peace and compromise with suspicion. On June 6, 1982, Israel, claiming that it intended to end attacks on its territory (although a cease-fire had been in effect since July 1981) and aiming to dislodge the PLO and encourage the installation of a Lebanese government friendly to Israel, launched an invasion of Lebanon. PLO and Syrian forces were defeated by

Israeli troops, and the remaining PLO forces were contained in West Beirut.

After a lengthy siege and bombardment by Israel in July and August 1982, some 11,000 Palestinian fighters were allowed to leave Beirut for various destinations, under international guarantees for their own safety and that of their civilian dependents. Despite these guarantees, however, after Israeli troops had occupied West Beirut, the Phalangists, Israel's rightist Lebanese allies, were allowed by Israeli forces into the Beirut refugee camps of Sabra and Shatila, where they massacred hundreds (estimates vary between 700 and 3,000) of Palestinian and Lebanese civilians.

Although not all PLO guerrillas were forced to leave Lebanon, the PLO infrastructure in the southern part of the country was destroyed, and Arafat's departure from Beirut to northern Lebanon marked the effective end of the PLO's military and political presence in the country. Ultimately, the new government of Lebanon came under the sway of Syria.

The dispersal of the PLO from Lebanon significantly weakened the organization's military strength and political militancy. It was unable to operate freely from any of the nation's bordering Israel. Arafat and the other PLO leaders were also threatened by the emergence within Fatah of a faction encouraged by Syria. In December 1983 Arafat was driven out of northern Lebanon by the Syrians and their protégés inside the PLO.

After having established himself near Tunis, Tunisia, Arafat turned once again to diplomatic initiatives. He sought Egyptian and Jordanian support against Syria. He also looked to King Ḥussein as an intermediary for negotiations with the United States and Israel that might lead to a Palestinian ministate on the West Bank within a Jordan-Palestine confederation an idea that had been favoured by the dominant factions in the PLO since the early 1980s. This policy was expressed most concretely in the meeting of the Palestine National Council in Amman in November 1984, the first time it had met there since Jordan had crushed the PLO armed forces in 1970.

Years of mounting violence

Violence escalated from the mid-1980s onward. Rejectionist elements within the PLO renewed their activities, attracting worldwide attention. In October 1985 members of the Palestine Liberation Front, a small faction within the PLO headed by Abū ʿAbbās, hijacked an Italian cruise ship, the Achille Lauro, and murdered one of its passengers. Following an Israeli bombing attack on PLO headquarters near Tunis several days before the hijacking, Arafat moved some departments to Saddam Hussein's Iraq. Lebanese Shīʿite Muslim groups fought the PLO to stop its reemergence as an armed rival for supremacy in the chaotic situation prevalent in West Beirut and southern Lebanon. West Bank Arabs demonstrated and engaged in strikes in late 1986.

In Israel several new developments strengthened Arab feelings of alienation from the Jewish majority. Ultranationalists increased their demands for more Jewish settlements and the annexation of the West Bank and advocated the forceful removal of the Palestinian Arabs from the occupied territories.

The Israeli parliament passed a bill in 1985 banning any political party that endangered state security i.e., any party that was anti-Zionist. This reinforced the feeling of most Israeli Arabs that no legal political party could adequately reflect their national, economic, and political views, although the only party actually banned was the anti-Arab Kach Party. Israelis especially West Bank settlers became more antagonistic and militant toward Palestinians as armed attacks against Israel and Israelis living abroad increased in number.

Throughout 1986–87 attacks by Arabs on Israeli settlers and by Israeli settlers on Arabs mounted. By 1988 more than half of the land in the West Bank and about a third of the land in the Gaza Strip had been transferred to Jewish control, and the Israeli population of the West Bank mostly concentrated in 15 metropolitan satellites of Tel Aviv–Yafo and Jerusalem had reached about 100,000.

By the late 1980s a whole generation of Palestinian youth had grown up under Israeli occupation. Nearly three-fourths of Palestinians were younger than 25 years of age. Their political status was uncertain, their civil rights diminished, and their economic status low and dependent on Israel's economy. Between 100,000 and 120,000 Palestinians crossed daily from the occupied territories into Israel to work.

They did not have much faith in Arab governments, nor did they place strong trust in the PLO, which, although still a powerful symbol of Palestinian aspirations, had not succeeded by either diplomatic or military efforts to win Palestinian self-determination. Remittances to family members left behind from those hundreds of thousands who had migrated to Jordan and the Persian Gulf states for work in the 1960s and '70s were reduced drastically as the economies of many Middle Eastern countries were hit by falling oil prices. Increasingly, Palestinians came to rely on their own efforts.

The intifadah

When the Palestinians saw no improvement in effective support of their aspirations from other countries and no likely favourable change coming from the Israelis, they engaged, throughout 1987, in small-scale demonstrations, riots, and occasional violence directed against Israelis. The Israeli authorities responded with university closings, arrests, and deportations. Large-scale riots and demonstrations broke out in the Gaza Strip in early December and continued for more than five years thereafter. This uprising, which became known as the intifadah (Arabic: "shaking off"), inspired a new era in Palestinian mass mobilization. Masked young demonstrators turned to throwing stones at Israeli troops, and the soldiers responded by shooting and arresting them. Women, and women's organizations, were prominent.

The persistent disturbances, initially spontaneous, before long came under the leadership of the Unified National Command of the Uprising, which had links to the PLO. The PLO soon incorporated the Unified Command, but not before the local leaders had pushed Arafat to abandon formally his commitment to armed struggle and to accept Israel and the notion of a two-state solution to the conflict.

One group, Ḥamās an acronym for the Islamic Resistance Movement challenged the authority of the secular nationalist movement, especially inside Gaza, and sought to take over the leadership of the intifadah. Ḥamās was an underground wing of the Muslim Brotherhood, which had built up a network of religious, educational, and charitable institutions in the occupied territories, in addition to establishing an armed wing known as the Sheikh ʿIzz al-Dīn al-Qassām Brigades (named for the nationalist leader killed by the British in 1935). Ḥamās rejected any accommodation with Israel.

Tactics and tolls

The tactics of the intifadah were highly sophisticated. Union-organized strikes, commercial boycotts and closures, and demonstrations were carried out in one part of the territories, and then, after Israel had reestablished its local power there, they were transferred to a previously quiescent area. Palestinian refugee camps provided major centers for the resistance, but Palestinian Arabs living in more affluent circumstances also participated, and some Israeli Arabs showed their sympathy with the goals of the uprising.

During its first year more than 300 Palestinians were killed, more than 11,500 wounded (nearly two-thirds of whom were under 15 years of age), and many more arrested. Israel closed universities and schools, destroyed houses, and imposed curfews yet it was unable to quell the uprising. By mid-1990 the International Red Cross estimated that more than 800 Palestinians had been killed by Israeli security forces, more than 200 of whom were under the age of 16. Some 16,000 Palestinians were in prison. By contrast, fewer than 50 Israelis had been killed. Some hundreds of Palestinians in the occupied territories, accused of being collaborators with Israel, were killed by their compatriots. Political paralysis gripped Israel.

PLO declaration of independence

Arafat sought to establish himself as the only leader who could unite and speak for the Palestinians, and in mid-1988 he took the diplomatic initiative. At the 19th session of the PNC, held near Algiers on November 12–15, 1988, he succeeded in having the council issue a declaration of independence for a state of Palestine in the West Bank and Gaza Strip. Arafat proclaimed the state (without defining its borders) on November 15. Within days more than 25 countries (including the Soviet Union and Egypt but excluding the United States and Israel) had extended recognition to the government-in-exile.

The final weeks of 1988 opened a new chapter in Palestinian-Israeli relations. In December Arafat announced that the PNC recognized Israel as a state in the region and condemned and rejected terrorism in all its forms including state terrorism, the PLO's term for

Israel's actions. He addressed a special meeting of the UN General Assembly convened at Geneva and proposed an international peace conference under UN auspices.

He publicly accepted UN resolutions 242 and 338, thereby recognizing, at least implicitly, the State of Israel. Despite their ambiguities, UN resolution 242 (1967), which encapsulated the principle of land for peace, and resolution 338 (1973), which called for direct negotiations, were regarded by both parties as the starting points for negotiations. Although Israeli Prime Minister Yitzhak Shamir stated that he was still not prepared to negotiate with the PLO, the U.S. government announced that it would open dialogue with the PLO.

The move toward self-rule

The approaching end of the Cold War left the Palestinians diplomatically isolated, as did PLO support for Iraqi President Saddam Hussein, who had invaded Kuwait in August 1990 but was defeated by a U.S.-led alliance in the Persian Gulf War (1990–91). Funds from Saudi Arabia, Kuwait, and the Persian Gulf states dried up. The Palestinian community in Kuwait, which had consisted of about 400,000 people, was reduced to a few thousand. Economic hardship was compounded by the fact that, during the continuing conflict along the Lebanese border and in the occupied territories, Israel imposed severe travel restrictions on Palestinian day labourers. The overall result was loss of jobs, loss of morale, and loss of support for the PLO leadership in Tunis.

However, prospects for a settlement of the outstanding issues between the Palestinians and Israel became significantly altered by several factors: the convening of an international peace conference between Israeli and Arab delegates (including Palestinians from the occupied territories as part of a joint Jordanian-Palestinian delegation) at Madrid in October 1991, sponsored by the United States and the Soviet Union (after December 1991, Russia); the dissolution of the Soviet Union in December; and the replacement, in the Israeli general elections of June 1992, of Shamir and the Likud-bloc government with a Labour Party government that was committed to implementing Palestinian autonomy within a year.

Although progress at the Madrid peace conference was discouraging, secret meetings held in Norway from January 1993 between PLO and Israeli officials produced an understanding known as the Oslo Accords. On this basis, on September 13, 1993, the PLO and Israel signed a historic Declaration of Principles in Washington, D.C. It included mutual recognition and terms whereby governing functions in the West Bank and Gaza would be progressively handed over to a

Palestinian Council for an interim period of five years, during which time Israel and the Palestinians would negotiate a permanent peace treaty to settle on the final status of the territories.

Despite acts of violence committed by extremist groups on both sides attempting to sabotage the peace process, the Israelis completed their withdrawal from the West Bank town of Jericho and parts of the Gaza Strip in May 1994. On July 1 Arafat entered Gaza in triumph. Four days later he swore in members of the Palestinian Authority (PA) in Jericho, which by the end of the year had assumed control of education and culture, social welfare, health, tourism, and taxation.

Violence and irreconcilable demands by radical elements in the populations of both sides obstructed talks between the PLO and the Israeli government. Nonetheless, on September 28, 1995, Arafat and Israeli Prime Minister Yitzhak Rabin and Foreign Minister

Shimon Peres signed an agreement in Washington providing for the expansion of Palestinian self-rule in the West Bank and for elections of a chairman and a legislative council of the PA.

The PA would gain control over six large West Bank towns (Janīn, Nāblus, Ṭūlkarm, Qalqīlyah, Ramallah, and Bethlehem) as well as control over most of Hebron. Israel would also gradually redeploy from some 440 villages, which would come under Palestinian rule. Security for those areas would rest with the Palestinian police, although Israeli military forces would be guaranteed freedom of movement throughout the area from which Israel redeployed. Reaffirming the commitment made in the 1993 peace accord, permanent-status negotiations were to be concluded by 1999.

In October 1995, as West Bank villages, towns, and cities were handed over to the PA, right-wing religious and extremist nationalist Israelis stepped up their rhetoric against Rabin and the peace process. On November 4, 1995, Israelis were stunned when Rabin was assassinated by a Jewish extremist. Peres, Rabin's successor, quickly expressed his determination to continue the planned Israeli deployments.

Elections were held in PA-administered areas in January 1996, in which about three-fourths of Palestinians of the West Bank and Gaza voted. Arafat secured nearly nine-tenths of the vote and assumed the presidency of the PA in February. He also remained chairman of the PLO. Fatah won 55 seats in the 88-seat legislative council. Ḥamās, however, did not participate in the election and continued its violent opposition to the peace process.

The progress toward peace was further cast into doubt when Benjamin Netanyahu, right-wing leader of the Likud Party, was elected prime minister of Israel in May

1996. Netanyahu left office following defeat at the hands of the Labour Party led by Ehud Barak in May 1999. Although Netanyahu reached some accords with the Palestinians, his term in office was marked by increasing mistrust between the two sides.

Subsequent events, however, were a disappointment to all concerned, as a number of negotiating deadlines passed without an agreement. Notable among these was the May 1999 date set as a deadline for a third stage of Israeli military redeployments, an end of the interim period, and a completion of "permanent status" talks on the most contentious issues such as the status of Jerusalem, the return of refugees, the presence of Israeli settlements in the occupied territories, and the issue of Palestinian sovereignty and statehood.

Also, after a decade of negotiating, eight of those years following the signing of the Declaration of Principles, less than one-fifth of the West Bank (in 15 isolated segments) and about two-thirds of the Gaza Strip had reverted to full Palestinian control. The rest remained under Israeli military occupation (combined with PA civil administration in some areas). The number of Israelis living in West Bank settlements (that now exceeded 150) had grown by some 80,000 in that period, and more Arab land had been confiscated in the occupied territories for expanding settlements and for constructing bypass roads reserved solely for use by Israelis.

Further, the gross domestic product per capita in Palestinian areas had actually declined in the nine years after the Madrid Peace Conference, Israel restricted the movement of Palestinians (and closed Jerusalem to West Bank and Gaza Strip Palestinians beginning in 1991), and accusations were widespread of corruption within the PA and of human rights abuses by its leaders. All of this made life for most residents of

PA-controlled areas worse, in many respects, than it had been before the peace process.

An Israeli-Palestinian summit meeting sponsored by the United States in July 2000 failed to resolve these outstanding issues and led only to an increasingly strained situation. In the aftermath of this summit, a visit to Jerusalem's Al-Ḥaram al-Sharīf (the Temple Mount) in September by Likud leader Ariel Sharon reviled by Palestinians for his role in the 1982 Sabra and Shatila massacres was the spark that set off a conflagration.

The visit was followed by demonstrations near Al-Aqṣā Mosque the next day, in which Israeli security forces killed and wounded dozens of Palestinian demonstrators. That was the signal for a renewed uprising, which reached a level of violence unseen in the first intifadah more than 1,000 died in its first 18 months, the overwhelming majority of them

Palestinian civilians and which engulfed the still largely occupied West Bank and Gaza Strip.

Thereafter, suicide bomb attacks by Palestinians in Israeli cities increased. Large numbers of Israelis, most of them civilians, were killed and wounded, and Israeli attacks on PA targets (most located within population centres) raised the already high casualty rate among the Palestinian populace. In the spring of 2002 Israeli troops reoccupied all the towns and cities of the West Bank, reclaiming security control from the PA and tightening restrictions on movement that had earlier been placed on Palestinian residents of the West Bank and Gaza Strip.

Negotiations reached a complete impasse, and the future of the occupied territories, and of relations between Palestinians and Israelis, became increasingly uncertain. Sharon, blaming Arafat for instigating the attacks against Israel, confined Arafat to his compound in Ramallah from 2001.

In 2003 the PA established the office of prime minister in an effort to circumvent Arafat and restart the peace process with Israel. Arafat installed Mahmoud Abbas, a moderate, in the post. Abbas called for an end to the intifadah, but, feeling that his efforts were thwarted by Arafat, Israel, and the United States, he soon resigned. Following Arafat's death in 2004, Abbas was elected chairman of the PLO and president of the PA. In 2005 Israel withdrew soldiers and settlers from parts of the West Bank and from all of the Gaza Strip, which then came under Palestinian control. The pullout raised hopes for new peace talks.

In the years that followed, tensions between Ḥamās and Fatah dominated Palestinian politics. Elections for the Palestinian Legislative Council were held in 2006, and Ḥamās won a surprise victory over Fatah. Ḥamās and Fatah eventually formed a coalition government, but violence between their forces escalated in the Gaza Strip. After a week of fighting, Ḥamās forces defeated Fatah forces and took control of the Gaza Strip, leading Abbas to dissolve the Ḥamās-led government and declare a state of emergency in June 2007.

The Ḥamās takeover of the Gaza Strip added a new element of uncertainty to Israeli-Palestinian relations. Israel declared the Gaza Strip under Ḥamās a hostile entity and imposed a blockade, sealing border crossings and placing heavy restrictions on imports. Ḥamās rocket attacks on southern Israel became commonplace, as did retaliatory strikes by Israeli forces.

Israel and Ḥamās agreed in June 2008 to a six-month cease-fire in negotiations brokered by Egypt. When the agreement expired in December, Ḥamās announced that it did not intend to extend it, and there were accusations of violations by both sides. A major conflict broke out in late December when Israel launched air strikes on Ḥamās targets in response to increased rocket attacks. A week after commencing the air strikes, Israel mounted a ground offensive into the Gaza Strip. The conflict ended after 22 days, with Israel and Ḥamās each declaring a unilateral cease-fire. Thirteen Israelis and more than 1,000 Gazans were killed in the fighting.

Relations between Israel and the Palestinians soured further in May 2010 when Israeli commandos raided a civilian ship carrying pro-Palestinian activists to the Gaza Strip in defiance of Israel's blockade. Nine people aboard the ship were killed when the commandos opened fire after being attacked by activists armed with clubs and knives. A round of direct peace talks between Israel and the PA was held in September 2010, but those talks quickly came to a halt over the construction of Israeli settlements in the West Bank.

After a four-year schism, during which Ḥamās and Fatah governed separately in the Gaza Strip and in the West Bank, respectively, Palestinian officials announced in April 2011 that Ḥamās and Fatah had reached a reconciliation agreement in negotiations mediated by Egypt. The plan, signed in Cairo on May 4, called for the formation of a caretaker government ahead of presidential and legislative elections to be held within a year.

Following the failure of direct talks in 2010, Abbas had shifted his efforts toward gaining international recognition for a Palestinian state. In September 2011 he submitted a request to the UN Security Council asking for the admission of an independent Palestinian state to the UN. The action which was opposed by Israel and the United States had become necessary, he argued, because the U.S.-mediated peace negotiations had placed too little pressure on Israel to make concessions for peace. The bid for recognition by the

Security Council stalled when it became clear that the United States would veto it and that several other members would abstain from voting.

A year after the failure of the Palestinian bid for full membership in the UN, Abbas announced that he would seek the UN General Assembly's implicit recognition of Palestinian statehood by submitting a draft resolution requesting that the status of the Palestinian mission to the UN (officially called Palestine within the UN) be upgraded from "permanent observer" to "nonmember observer state." The designation, though falling short of full UN membership, would allow Palestinians to seek membership in international bodies such as the International Criminal Court. The resolution passed on November 29, 2012, with 138 countries in favour, 9 opposed, and 41 abstentions. The resolution also urged Israel and the Palestinians to resume stalled negotiations toward a two-state solution. Israeli officials opposed Abbas's bid for recognition, saying that such unilateral actions by the Palestinians would hold up negotiations with Israel.

The murders of three teenage yeshiva students in the West Bank in June 2014 for which Netanyahu held Ḥamās responsible brought a new escalation of tension in and around the Gaza Strip. On July 8, 2014, Israel launched a large-scale attack against Ḥamās and other militants in Gaza that began with a week of aerial bombardment and progressed to an incursion by ground troops. After several weeks of fighting, Israel withdrew its forces from the Gaza Strip, declaring that their mission had been fulfilled.

www.ingramcontent.com/pod-product-compliance
Lightning Source LLC
Chambersburg PA
CBHW021102080526
44587CB00010B/344